P9-DHB-875

GOOD · OLD · DAYS
On the Farm ™

HOUSE of
WHITE
BIRCHES
PUBLISHERS
SINCE 1947

GOOD·OLD·DAYS
On the Farm™

Copyright © 1996 House of White Birches, Berne, Indiana 46711

All rights reserved. No part of this publication may be reproduced or
transmitted in any form or by any means, electronic or mechanical,
including photocopying, recording, or any other information storage
and retrieval system, without the written permission of the publisher.

Editor: Ken Tate
Associate Editor: Janice Tate
Editorial Director: Vivian Rothe

Production Manager: Vicki Macy
Design/Production Artist: Barb Knepple
Creative Coordinator: Shaun Venish
Production Coordinator: Sandra Beres
Production Assistants: Carol Dailey,
Cheryl Lynch, Chad Tate
Copy Editor: Läna Schurb

Publishers: Carl H. Muselman, Arthur K. Muselman
Chief Executive Officer: John Robinson
Marketing Director: Scott Moss

Printed in the United States of America
First Printing: 1996
Library of Congress Number: 96-76084
ISBN: 1-882138-19-8

Every effort has been made to ensure the accuracy of the material
in this book. However, the publisher is not responsible for human error
or typographical mistakes in this publication.

Dear Friends of the Good Old Days,

When I think of the Good Old Days, my first thoughts turn back to the farm. Like many of you, I was raised on the farm—ours was on a rocky hilltop in the Ozark Mountains of southern Missouri. In those days there wasn't much money, but if you lived on the farm—well, you just didn't miss it as much.

Daddy had cattle; it was no dairy operation, but we milked for a bit of money from the local cheese factory. Since we didn't have electricity in the early years—and only had it at the house in later years—we didn't have the luxury of milking machines. Still, we always had fresh milk to drink, and meat at butchering time.

Grandma and Mama raised chickens. They sold eggs and fryers to help make ends meet. Our garden was usually abundant, if the Lord provided enough rain to water it. Each summer was a race to put up as much fruit and vegetables as we could before the drought of late July and August baked the garden spot into nothingness. It was hot, hard work—but how good those jars of God-given sustenance were come the snows of winter!

Looking back today, I find two big truths from my early life of those days down on the farm.

First, the world was much bigger then. As I grew older and my world expanded, I came to realize the 40 or so acres we shared communally with my grandmother and Uncle Bob was really a fairly small patch of land.

Second, I came to realize that riches are a state of mind. I always thought we were rich. We had food when some were hungry. We didn't have much money, but we didn't have much to spend it on either.

But we *were* rich! We had a strong family and good health. We had plenty of food and a good feather bed to sleep in at night. We had more than a skinny young kid could ever imagine having. I thank God every day for these memories of the Good Old Days down on the farm.

Sincerely,

Ken Tate

Editor

Contents

AUTUMN DAYS • 97

WINTER DAYS • 133

John
Slobodnik

Springtime Memories

Every year as March rolls around I look forward to another planting season. Janice and I don't plant as much as we once did, but a year without fresh vegetables and a summer without the old canner putting off a few quarts of green beans, beets and pickles would be like a winter without Christmas—time would go on, but without the joy and peace simple things bring to our lives.

I come from a long line of planters, hoers and weeders. Grandma and Grandpa Tate had a garden until the last few years of their lives. When they no longer could garden, Daddy and his siblings made sure they were stocked with more produce than they could handle.

Likewise, Mama and Daddy continued to garden well into their 70s. But as the years passed, I watched as the old garden spot dwindled with each departing child. Finally it was a small rectangle of rich soil about 15 by 20 feet in size—about the size of my garden spot today. Mama and Daddy used Dan and Jibe, Grandma Stamps' work horses, to plow with. I learned to handle the pair when they were old enough—and tired enough—not to give a youngster a lot of trouble.

Janice and I, in later years, were fortunate enough to have a tractor to break our huge garden. That was when the kids were growing up—and eating like it. But, like both our sets of parents, our needs diminished and so did the size of the ground we planted. Now all we need is a good tiller.

One need, however, never has diminished, and I hope it never does as long as I draw breath. That is the need for me to see things grow. It is like the renewal of a miracle every year as the seeds we plant sprout, break to the surface, spread verdant leaves to the sun and sky, then provide a fresh crop of delicacies to sustain us—and give us pleasure.

It reminds me of every kitten or puppy I held as a child. Of every calf I helped deliver as a young man. Of every child Janice and I brought into life, cultivated in the ways of the world, then prayerfully and tearfully watched as they took root and bore fruit. Life, like a good garden, can be a tough row to hoe—but when you are able to enjoy the fruit of your labor, it isn't that bad.

This year I'll probably plant too much again. I'll put too many potatoes in the ground. After the last frost, a little later in the spring, I'll plant too many tomatoes (my favorite). My row of beans will be too long and there will be too many beets and radishes and too much lettuce. Janice will have to hear me complain about the size of the garden again—but she will know I don't really mean it.

Like all born planters, hoers and weeders, I'll just get another tube of Ben-Gay for my back, grab my garden tools and go find me a long row to hoe. It's just one of those habits—and pleasures—left over from spring on the farm in the Good Old Days.

—Ken Tate

Nine Is Old Enough!

By Chet Nolte

When I was 9, my dad decided that I was old enough and big enough to handle a team in the cornfield. This decision was not entirely accepted by my mother, who thought I should wait another year or so to take on the responsibilities of an adult.

"Give the lad a little more time to grow and he'll be that much better a hand," she cautioned. But Dad was persistent, and finally it was decided that I should get a trial to see whether I could perform as Dad thought I could.

In those days, we plowed corn with single-row cultivators, most of which had three shovels on each side of the row of corn.

It was a sure bet I couldn't operate a shovel-plow, but there was one plow I could probably work with, and it was called a "surface culti-vator" from the way it was constructed.

This plow had sweeps instead of shovels, which ran along just under the ground, the dirt flowing over their flat surfaces in such a way as to do what shovel plows did but without digging so deep.

Another feature of the plow was that its two sides, unlike the shovel plows of that day, were bolted together so that one movement of the stirrups would move both of the opposing gangs to the right or left as needed. The object was to keep the row of corn in the middle of the two front sweeps. Failure to keep the row centered might result in cutting off the young corn instead of the weeds and grass between the rows.

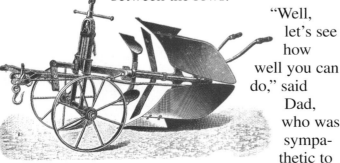

"Well, let's see how well you can do," said Dad, who was sympathetic to my first try at plowing. He had harnessed Old Bess and Bird, a truly mild-mannered older team, who could be counted on to know the ropes and not cause any trouble in the field.

It was a hot day in June, and we were about to start over the first time. The horses moved between the rows at a very slow walk; the reins were knotted over one shoulder and under my other arm. By moving my shoulders, I soon learned to guide the team in the direction I wanted them to go. But keeping the row centered between the sweeps was quite another matter.

Success in surface plowing depended on leg strength to move the two clone-like gangs from side to side. There was, however, a limit to how far they could go. I have to confess, I did sacrifice a few small corn plants before I got the hang of steering the team and keeping the sweeps centered. Dad was proud of the way I got along and he triumphantly announced at noon dinner that "He's doing the work of a grown man," which did a lot to help my insecurity in the new task.

Years later I was to learn there was such a thing as "child labor laws," but on the farm it seemed only natural to hold up my end of the task. Working together as a family was the mode among farm families of the time, and nobody thought anything about it. Dad was always careful not to overwork us, and we felt we were doing something important and necessary to our way of life. I wonder how many kids today would take up the slack at age 9?

What greater gift can a father leave his son than a love for the soil and the inner feeling that he is important in the scheme of life? I will always say that nothing is more valuable than the feeling instilled in a young person that his life is sustaining to others. And when does that feeling begin? I'd say, along about 9. ❖

Mama's Chickens

By Reta Mae Johnson

During quite a number of stormy nights in early spring, I found my way downstairs to finish the night with Mama, safe and unafraid, on the couch. Mama was sleeping downstairs on the couch because it was baby chick time in the '20s. Two coal-oil–heated incubators, each warming about 200 "home-grown" eggs, filled one-third of the front room.

During the daytime, Mama let my two sisters and me help mark each egg with a little laundry bluing. Two times each day, every egg was turned over—all bluing showing at night and none during the day. A tiny thermometer showed the temperature inside the incubator to be 103 degrees.

The routine was broken during the second week when we candled the eggs. For this chore, Mama pulled the trays of eggs to the front of the incubator and passed the flashlight under each egg, one at a time. If the egg was dark, all was well. But if it seemed light, that meant it wasn't fertile so out it went.

At the end of three weeks things began to happen! We would find a few pipped eggs—the baby chick breaking the shell for entry into the world. The next morning, sure enough, a few fluffy bits of chicken with dark little eyes were among other eggs in the trays. Soon the trays were full.

These little balls of fluff housed in cardboard boxes had to share the kitchen with Mama, Dad and us three girls. We had no brooder house, so this was the warmest place for them. On sunshiny days, we put them outside in temporary pens; on cold rainy days, they chirped forlornly from their boxes in the kitchen. Behind the cookstove, a warm box with soft cloth lining was hospital for the not-so-hardy ones.

Crows and chicken hawks thought baby chicks fine fare, so my sister Maxine and I spent many hours playing near the chicken pens to scare them away.

One day Dad took a few of the "hopelessly hospitalized" chicks with him when he went back to the field to plow. He climbed up the hedge tree, removed the eggs from the crow's nest and put the sick chicks in. Every day he climbed up to check them. All was well for about a week; then he found the nest empty. Perhaps the old crow decided they were foreigners and ate them for lunch.

The very finest roosters were kept for next year's flock but the others ended up on the table. Mama would toss down a handful or two of corn and grab the foolish roosters who came for a few grains. She'd quickly remove Mr. Rooster's head. After a bit of flopping around on the ground, he lay still. A bucket of hot water loosened the feathers and he was soon cleaned, in the skillet and filling the air with the aroma of fried chicken.

The hens were kept for laying eggs, which we sold each week—dozens and dozens of them—to Dawson Produce in Bronson, Kan.

During the Depression years the chickens were our means of survival. When things got really bad, Dad would cull a dozen or so hens who were not laying eggs, tie their legs together with baling twine, put them between the front and back seats of the Model-T and haul them into town. This money bought flour, coal oil, shoes or whatever was absolutely necessary. Nothing was charged—ever!

Today, I have a few chickens for fertilizer and the pleasure of caring for them. But sometimes when I turn them out of the henhouses, I can close my eyes and be a little girl again, turning Mama's fine laying hens out for their day in the sun. They helped us survive. ❖

Crows and chicken hawks thought baby chicks fine fare, so my sister Maxine and I spent many hours playing near the chicken pens to scare them away.

Early Days on the Farm

By Max M. Keller

was born a short distance from our family farm in 1905. It was in south central Illinois near the small town of Kinmundy, the only town in the United States by that name. I believe there is a settlement or village in Scotland by the same name. We used to say, "We can't do it today, but we Kinmundy" (can Monday).

My parents bought the farm in 1906 and lived there all their lives. I can recall many pleasant experiences here as a farm boy growing up in the country: going out through the fields and woods with my yellow shepherd dog, climbing the tallest trees, and in wintertime hunting rabbits and quail. I was the oldest of three children, having two sisters, two and four years younger.

My father was a farmer who also operated a country store and gristmill at the farm. He hired a man to help with farm work year-round as the store and mill took most of his time. The store was a typical country store, with the cracker barrel, candy in wooden pails or tubs, plug tobacco cut with the long-handled tobacco knife (which I still have), the wood heating stove in the center of the store, a cash drawer which pulled out from under the counter, etc.

The gristmill operated with a 10-horsepower gasoline engine that sat outside the building on a large concrete foundation. The engine had two flywheels about 5 feet in diameter, and to start it we had to spin the wheels by hand until it kicked off. This mill had a set of French burrs on which cornmeal, wheat and buckwheat flour were ground.

During World War I there was no rationing of food items, but Uncle Sam made a plea for all to be conservative so that the doughboys would have the best. One item to conserve was flour. In those days people wanted to be patriotic, so those who had wheat would bring it to my father's mill. He

Like most farm boys, I had chores to do as well as take a hand in farming. The most pleasant job was during haying— mowing or cutting the hay down.

JAY KILLIAN

ground it and had bolters to take the bran out, thereby making a fairly white flour. My mother used this home-ground flour to make biscuits each morning..

Like most farm boys, I had chores to do as well as take a hand in farming. Most of the farming implements were walking tools. The most pleasant job was during haying—mowing or cutting the hay down. I did like to ride the horse-drawn mower and watch the red-top hay fall behind the sickle. This particular kind of hay was profitable because of the red-top seed which, when threshed out, had a good market. The most disliked job, which fell to my lot,

was operating the sweep rake, sometimes called the bull rake. It was so wide, with a horse on one side and another horse on the other side, that it was hard to drive them and keep the rake going forward evenly.

In 1916 my father bought his first car—a Model-T Ford with a brass radiator. What a thrill it was to go places in an automobile! In winter, though, we had to revert back to the buggy or wagon, because in those days there were no improved roads in the country.

I think back to the good home I was reared in, with a father and mother who loved us children and showed it as long as they lived. ❖

Saturday's Child

By Ruby L. Anders

Each child in our family had a specific chore to do on Saturday before he was free to enjoy his own pursuits.

The older boys did chores around the barn while 10-year-old Carl filled the wood box on the porch.

Myra's job was to clean the corner cupboard in the dining room where Mama kept the good china. Myra actually enjoyed her job of handling the fragile china that was painted with red roses and green leaves. We all knew the story of how the china came clear across three states in a barrel of flour in a covered wagon driven by our grandfather. Our grandmother, it seems, had hidden the china in the flour without Grandpa's knowledge.

Myra also loved to clean the tall thin goblets that Papa had bought Mama as a surprise one time when he took the cattle into the city to market. Carefully she wiped out the tall goblets with the gold bands and carefully she put fresh paper on the shelves before returning the dishes to their places.

Kate dusted every piece of furniture with O'Cedar furniture polish until you could see yourself in it, and Mary Nelle polished mirrors and lamp chimneys until they gleamed.

I gladly would have traded jobs with any of them because my Saturday job was to clean the huge black cookstove that graced the corner of our kitchen. Mother was strict about that stove, vowing it would have to last a lifetime.

The Home Comfort, as the stove was called, was our only source of heat for cooking and heating the kitchen and dining room. The stove was appreciated most of all in winter on Saturday nights when the tub was brought in for our weekly baths. But to me, who had to clean it, it looked like a black monster, and every Saturday I eyed it with loathing. I particularly hated the job because, while the others could be finished with their tasks by noon, I had to wait until the stove had cooled off after Mama's Saturday baking and the midday meal.

First I shook down the wood ashes. We had lots of timber so we didn't burn coal. I emptied the ashes outside in the chicken lot so the chickens could scratch in them. Then I dipped out any water left in the reservoir attached to the side of the stove and wiped it clean.

Next, I lifted the nickel-plated trim from the front of the stove and polished it with Bon-Ami. The warming oven with the pipe running through it had to be washed with sudsy water and carefully dried to prevent rusting.

Then I was ready for the stove polish, and I always finished with a good supply of it under my fingernails. It didn't come out until I had washed my hands several times. I always tried to keep my hands hidden at Sunday school.

While the polish dried, I filled the reservoir with fresh water and laid a fire for the evening meal. Then, with a cloth, I polished the stove.

With relief I replaced the nickel-plated trim, washed my hands and stood by impatiently while Mama inspected the stove. When she smiled her approval and gave me a couple of fresh baked cookies, I was free to go join my friend Ruth to enjoy what was left of the Saturday afternoon.

But it wasn't until after Myra got married and I inherited her job and Kate took over the stove that I realized it wasn't such a bad job and more in my line. Somehow, handling that china gave me the willies and I was glad to pass it on to the next in line. ❖

Taking Off the "Diddies"

By Myrtle T. Aldridge

By early spring the hens had "laid out their litter" (of eggs) and wanted to set. They would take to a nest with more determination than a lop-eared mule in his dash for the barn and a good feed.

Mama usually put eggs under the hens and let them set to their heart's content. We knew that a portion of the roosters would wind up as platters of golden fried chicken. Others would be swapped for household necessities when the peddler made his weekly rounds.

One spring Mama had set several hens the same evening (there was some significance about putting the eggs under the hens at sundown). She kept reminding Papa that she would need new chicken coops, as the old ones had fallen into decay.

Papa was busy with the spring planting and kept saying, "Oh, well, I'll get to it in due time."

Finally it was past due time. When Papa came to the house for the noonday meal, Mama told him that the baby chickens—which we called "little diddies"—had hatched and three had fallen out of the nest by the side of the smokehouse.

As soon as the meal was over, Papa grudgingly set about his task. He nailed up a long structure with partitions so that each hen could have an apartment for her brood.

My 5-year-old sister eagerly watched each step of the construction. Finally she leaned over Papa's shoulder and asked, "How many rooms are you going to make, Papa?"

"Fifteen and a front porch," he drily answered.

When he finished the chicken coop and got back to his plowing, Mama set about getting the hens and their broods settled in. She would put the little diddies in her apron while the mama hen squawked and carried on. Then she

Look into the Future!

POULTRY PROFITS at this season are in the future. Time only will tell whether you hatch 50%, 75% or more chicks.

Past records for years prove that eggs from breeders fed Purina Poultry Chows hatch more chicks and better chicks—with greater profit.

That's why hundreds of thousands of poultry raisers will again depend on Purina in Checkerboard bags this spring—for breeders and baby chicks. Order Purina Poultry Chows from the store with the checkerboard sign. Feed breeders Purina Poultry Chows for at least thirty days before beginning to save hatching eggs.

Write for the new 96-page 1927 Purina Poultry Book—Free

PURINA MILLS
840 Gratiot Street
St. Louis, Mo.
*Seven Busy Mills
Located for Service*

PURINA CHICKEN CHOWDER

PURINA HEN CHOW (SCRATCH FEED)

would get the hen under her other arm and head for the coop.

One old hen was extra fussy. She made so much noise it attracted the biggest rooster in the yard. He came running and circled around Mama a few times, giving out warning noises as if to say, "This is my domain."

Mama ignored him completely. Finally he rose from the ground and pecked Mama between the shoulders. She let go of the diddies she was holding, whirled and caught the rooster. She took him by the neck and pitched him over in the grass, exclaiming, "There! I guess that'll learn you not to peck me, sir!" Later he made pretty good rooster and dumplings.❖

Outhouses Can Be Beautiful

By Susan Hatch Tayler

April brought dogwood blossoms, sparrows and gentle rain to the small farming community of O'Neill Ridge. It also brought that most dreaded of all farm chores—spring cleaning.

Inside the farmhouses, women took up their carpets, then lugged them outside to be hung over clotheslines. The youngsters then spent hours beating the dust out of those carpets with brooms or carpet beaters. Floors were scrubbed and waxed until they shone. Closets and attics were cleaned out and surplus goods put out to await the arrival of the junk dealer.

Then the men began painting. The inside of the house came first, then the outside. Last, but certainly not least, the big barn got its annual coat of bright red paint. Finally it was done.

The following Saturday, Abby Balson, age 6, and her 12-year-old cousin, Roxanne, were left alone at the farm while Abby's folks went to town. They didn't have any chores to do and had been told to "Have fun and don't get into trouble."

Roxanne decided to bake a pie for supper and so Abby went for a walk. On her tour of the farm, she discovered that everything looked so pretty after the spring cleaning—everything, that is, except the outhouse.

Now, their farm was set on a curved road so that when a visitor came from town, the outhouse was the first sight he saw. Abby figured that Papa had just forgotten to paint it and she would help him out.

She found two cans of paint in the tool shed. One was the same blue as her bedroom and the other was red barn paint. She got to work. It took her all day but finally she got done. How she climbed the ladder with all her gear, no one will ever know. She was so tired that she was in bed, sound asleep, by the time her folks got home.

Now Papa usually didn't bother to take a lantern when he visited the out-house and tonight was no exception.

When he opened the door, the smell of wet paint greeted him and upon sitting down he discovered that someone had indeed painted the outhouse—walls, floors and toilet seat.

He was furious! You could hear him yell clear back to the house. He later found out that his backside was the most gorgeous red you have ever seen!

Abby had painted the inside with the barn paint which takes a whole week to dry. The outside she had done in blue and red stripes. It was the talk of the town for a long time to come. Needless to say, Abby's behind was red the next day—but not from paint. ✤

The Old-Fashioned Washtub

By Mrs. Joyce Bennett

In the "good old days" one wasn't so richly blessed with so many luxuries, so even getting something as modest in value as a galvanized washtub put the "good" in the old days.

My husband had gotten out of the service and we lived and worked in partnership with his folks for about a year and a half, all this time looking for a small nearby farm of our own,.

One spring day we were driving around the neighborhood and saw a little old man at his run-down farm. We stopped for a visit and the next thing we knew, we had rented ourselves a farm. The house hadn't been lived in for several years, and how tickled Old Man Johnson was to have it rented to an ambitious couple! The porches were crumbling, and there were shingles missing here and there. The outside hadn't had any paint for many a year, so we gave it the name of the Old Black House.

Some areas on the walls needed as much as three feet of plaster, and the paper hung down like the torn, grimy, gray arms of a beggar's coat, falling to the floor to lay among the crumbling plaster and cobwebs. It took many pails of sweepings before we could even plaster the walls and scrub the floors. Then came the wallpapering.

We both had watched our mothers paper, but of course had never helped. First we put the paste on too thick and each strip was so wet and heavy it tore before it got even to the ceiling. We had to laugh as each wet strip settled on our heads. Then came the painting, and the interior of the house was like new. But the outside of the old frame house remained black.

How happy I was to see the new shipment of galvanized tubs, and happy, too, I had $2 for one after buying the necessary staples

Our small savings covered only a dinette set and a good stove, so we made do with a lot of hand-me-downs, such as the old kitchen cabinet which I repainted, adding a tulip on each door, as I also did on the white oilcloth curtains. My mother had taught me to always add my own personal touch to something old, and it would seem like new.

Mother Bennett had a new Maytag washing machine, so I inherited her old one. Being a city girl, it took some getting used to the old ways of Grandma's on the farm. As we had no electricity, the washer had a motor one had to tromp on several times to start. There was no refrigerator, of course, as there was no available ice when one lived on a farm several miles from the nearest town, but there was a dandy brick cave out back of the house.

Washdays aren't too bad, I thought as I pumped a dozen pails of water and carried them about a half-block to fill the copper boiler on the range. It took about an hour to heat up good, so that gave me time to bake cookies and to put a pot of beans on to simmer slowly on the back of the stove. (Jim used to ask why we had to have navy beans every washday. Well, since both mothers did this to conserve fuel, so did I.) After the water was carried to the back porch to the washer, I used the boiler for a rinse tub.Wasn't very handy, but like I said before, we both had to make do until we couldafford something better.

One Saturday, as usual, we took our crate of eggs in to the small general store. Mr. Jensen had just about anything one wanted in the line of hardware, besides his well-stocked grocery shelves. How happy I was to see the new shipment of galvanized tubs, and happy, too, I had $2 for one after buying the necessary staples and a sack of laying mash for the hens. The hens came first, and this was a good policy as the egg money was our only source of income at the time.

The next washday was a breeze. I was out hanging up the first load when I heard my baby, Cherie, giggling. There she was, sitting in the water. "Swimmin', Mommy," she said. It took some convincing to have her wait until I had finished with the wash. Then, while she napped, the shiny new tub was sitting out in the sun, warming fresh water for her. She was one happy kid, and I'm sure Mr. Tub was happy, too.

This became almost a daily chore for him, except on the days it rained, and it did often in the spring in Iowa, so on those days he sat on the back step and caught the rain water. Even rain was a precious thing to save, for soft water sure saved on the amount of soap one used.

Summer days on a farm were the longest and hardest, but the most productive. Many tubfuls of tomatoes were picked and hauled to the kitchen to be canned. Mr. Tub carried in sweet corn and cucumbers, too.

Another spring came, and with it oat sowing time. Jim came running in to get the big tub for the clover seed and me to keep the seed hopper full. He had put the tub on top of the oats in the wagon, and baby Cherie and I sat on the oats for the roughest ride of all. This way a field could be seeded with oats and clover at the same time. If this sounds confusing to the city folks, I'd better explain that the oats grew so fast that they were harvested long before clover had poked up its lazy heads.

The clover yielded better than the oats crop, and after paying off the note at the bank, we were able to get several things for the farm and

I WISH I WAS JELT DENIM—STARCH AND FILLER CAN'T TAKE THE PLACE OF EXTRA YARN!

WATCH THOSE Lee OVERALLS GO!

JELT DENIM HOLDS FULL WEARING STRENGTH THROUGH WASHING AFTER WASHING!

EXTRA YARN CAN'T BE WASHED OUT... CUTS SHRINKAGE AMAZINGLY ... GIVES MONTHS LONGER WEAR!

1716 EXTRA FEET OF YARN IN EVERY PAIR

IT doesn't take many washings to show up the weakness in ordinary "bargain" overalls. Starch and fillers soon wash out, leaving them thin and flimsy—mere ghosts of what they were. Rips, tears and worn spots follow fast—soon you're buying overalls again.

None of that in Lee Overalls! They're made of JELT DENIM with 1716 extra feet of yarn in every pair. That's why Lee Overalls go through washing after washing without getting thin. Their body is woven—not starched in. That tighter, firmer weave also means greatly reduced shrinkage. It makes a stronger fabric, too—far greater protection against snags, rips and tears. It eliminates weak spots and gives MONTHS LONGER WEAR in every garment.

That's what you get in Lees alone, because no other overall is made of JELT Denim. But you get far more than that in Lees—22 special features—which add immensely to your comfort and convenience. Others may give you some of these features, but only Lees give you every one in every pair!

But, remember, there's only one way to be sure you are getting all these values and the money-saving longer wear of JELT Denim besides. Insist on getting Lees and accept no substitutes!

The H. D. Lee Merc. Company
Dept. M-11
Kansas City, Mo.   Trenton, N. J.   South Bend, Ind.
Minneapolis, Minn.   San Francisco, Calif.
Salina, Kan.

GUARANTEE
If you don't find Lee Overalls the longest-wearing overalls you have ever worn, you can get a new pair free or your money back.

UNION-MADE "Just Like Dad's"

Lee OVERALLS

UNION-ALLS, SHIRTS, PANTS, PLAY SUITS

Mail Coupon for Free Sample of JELT DENIM

THE H. D. LEE MERC. CO., Dept. M-11
Kansas City, Mo.
Kindly send me free sample of JELT Denim and name of nearest dealer handling Lee Overalls.

Name ....
Address ....
City .... State ....

NRA CODE

DEALERS
Write for sample plan through which your overall department benefits your entire business. Thousands of merchants have found it amazingly effective.

always runts, who get pushed away from Mama's table. (She has just so many plates to go around!) Dad brought in six little scrawny ones and put them in the big tub with a lot of straw for bedding. It was my job to bottle-feed them every few hours with a baby bottle, and you know, they were like babies—demanding at 2 a.m. feeding, too! And my, what a racket on the back porch until the last one was fed.

I was very glad they grew so fast. In a couple of weeks they could be weaned from the bottle to a pan and taken out to a shed. We saved every one, and I was pleased to see them go off to market with the others. I think the tub sighed a sigh of relief, too.

After a good scrub-down, Mr. Tub went back to the lawn to warm up the water for the youngsters. They called him their swimming pool now. Some weekends he sat under the pump filled with cold water, chilling a huge watermelon. Other times, when we had company, we loved to make homemade ice cream. The tub was used for this, too, filled with crushed ice, and the freezer put in. It was a hand-crank type, of course; we still hadn't got electricity in the early '50s.

The tomatoes did real well that year, and I even ran out of jars, for I had canned 50 quarts of bread-and-butter pickles besides the usual dills. We went over to an old neighbor whose

the house, too. Hubby surprised me with a new washer. My old one had broken down again, and with a new baby, all it seemed I got done was washing clothes on the scrub board and using the soaking method. The machine came with a set of rinse tubs, and I bet Mr. Tub thought he could loaf on the back porch more than ever. Oh, how mistaken he was, for on the farm he became busier than ever. Summer days meant a garden, and all those vegetables he had to carry in again.

The sows were having their baby pigs, a record crop. When they have so many there are canning days were over, and she sold us about a hundred jars for a penny apiece. So that year I was able to hit my goal of a hundred quarts of tomatoes in juice, sauce and ketchup.

The kids and I would go back to the "back forty" and get the sweet corn, pulling the big red wagon with the tub on top. Many a trip was made this way. Daddy was doing custom combining. The kids thought it a treat to have corn on the cob so often. To get them to really help me rake up the lawn, I'd promise them a picnic afterward; one never saw such workers. We piled the leaves into the old tub and pulled it on the wagon again to the back yard where we had a bonfire. We roasted wieners and toasted marshmallows by the bagful.

In the fall, it was time to pick the pears. We had such a huge tree that one year I climbed all over that tree and ended up with 30 bushels. These we hauled—in the tub on the wagon again—to the back porch where I wrapped several real green ones in newspaper and put them away for late-winter treats.

Finally winter came, and with it a rest for the farmer and his wife. Also, the busy tub got to sleep behind the wood-burning stove, holding the dry kindling and cobs.

No television in those days for us; our long evenings were spent listening to the battery-operated radio and reading countless books and magazines. It was fun, too, just to sit in front of the hot stove, eating popcorn and pears. Also, we had a bushel of red Jonathan apples. This was considered a luxury, which we indulged in every year. The kids would have their hot cocoa with marshmallows floating on top.

One cold, rainy March day, Jim had been out all morning searching for Mable, the cow. She had run off somewhere to have her calf. By the time he had found her and the new calf, the rain had turned to sleet. The calf was covered with ice and was too heavy, besides, to carry alone, so he came running in to get me and shook the old tub awake, dumping out the cobs into a bushel basket.

We rushed out as fast as one can walk on a sheet of ice, knowing that every minute counted. It was about half a mile to the corner of the pasture. What a job it was, with that squirming critter. Back home I quickly rubbed him down with towels and Jim put him on the oven door to sleep on a braided rug, more dead than alive.

"Well, doubt it if he even makes it, but we sure tried, didn't we, Ma?" he said, and went out to finish the chores. The kids and I had a surprise for him when he came in, for he was greeted by happy shouts as we tried to hold down the wild creature, scampering around the kitchen. He grew into a dandy steer that summer.

Poor old tub; it seemed he had just fallen asleep when he was once again shook free of his cobs. It was oat-sowing time again, and he would be used for the clover seed. He must have thought of all the summer work ahead, for he truly was my right-hand man. He had stuck with us through thick and thin and still didn't leak.

But now, after 15 years as tenant farmers, we just never seemed to get ahead, so we decided to quit and have a farm sale. Since we were moving clear to Wyoming, we sold almost everything except our clothes and personal belongings.

I remember the old tub brought $2, the very same price we'd paid for it new. After our move, we purchased a small tub for the dog's bath. On inspection, Hubby said, "Remember that big tub that lasted all our farm years? Well, they sure don't build them like they used to."

And I agreed, remembering all those chores he had helped me with. He sure did deserve a good rest and is probably snoozing in an antique shop back home, after all these years. ✣

1,250 Pounds of Ornery

By Bill Presto

Almost any dirt farmer who worked mules at one time or another had at least one named Jack. My granddad so named a mule he received in a horse trade. Ol' Jack, like all mules, had his own distinct personality that would have tried the patience of Job.

The intelligent look in the eyes of this 2-year-old mule veiled the lurking mischief. The profound arrogance in his walk proclaimed his free and independent spirit. Even after a hard day's work, he was forever lifting his flared nostrils to sniff the air and bray defiantly.

On one occasion shortly after Ol' Jack came to stay with us, Granddad sat in the corn crib shucking corn and piling it into a feed basket. Ol' Jack eyed Granddad with an indulgent show of resentment that was to become his trademark.

Granddad finished shucking the corn. Ol' Jack engaged in what eventually became his favorite form of mischief: He caught Granddad with his back turned and bit him. In return, Ol' Jack got a blow to the head with the feed basket. It hardly fazed the mule, for he nonchalantly barged his way under the feed shed. Granddad heaped a few well-chosen adjectives upon Ol' Jack, but they, too, fell upon an indifferent mind.

The following day, as Granddad attempted to hook the trace chains to the singletree, Ol' Jack broke loose and took off like a blue streak across the open field. Granddad finally caught the mule, hooked him to the plow, and the remainder of the day was spent in mutual animosity.

That evening Ol' Jack finished his ration of corn and, tired though he must have been, tore through the open gate and raced around the pasture in a frolicking display of temperament.

The months ahead brought no change in Ol' Jack's exhibitions of independence. A constant surveillance of Ol' Jack's ears was necessary. Months became years. Ol' Jack and Granddad just could not seem to reach an understanding.

Granddad's patience wore thinner with each annoyance. Take Grandmother's pear tree, for example. Ol' Jack had seen that big old pear tree many times in the center of the vegetable garden. The garden was a forbidden area for Ol' Jack and he knew it.

The intelligent look in the eyes of this 2-year-old mule veiled the lurking mischief. The profound arrogance in his walk proclaimed his free and independent spirit.

One Saturday at noon, after finishing a morning of plowing, Ol' Jack was turned out to pasture for his weekend of rest. He walked through the pasture alleyway, grazing the grass along the fence beside the garden.

Granddad had just begun his bath when he was startled by a crash coming from the garden. Quickly, he donned a pair of overalls and rushed to see the cause of the commotion. There, majestically standing in the middle of the garden, was Ol' Jack, munching pears on the tree's lower limbs.

Granddad grabbed a stick and drove him out of the garden with a liberal sprinkling of precise adjectives which, of course, fell on deaf ears—Ol' Jack was not perturbed in the slightest.

But Granddad was a man of great compassion. He decided if Ol' Jack was so determined to enjoy the taste of half-ripe pears, then he should have them. Granddad gathered about a dozen of the pears and put them in the horse trough so that Ol' Jack could enjoy them at his leisure. A week passed. The pears remained untouched. The sport had been taken out of it and he did not want any part of them.

Finally Granddad's patience wore out. He determined to sell him. Word of Ol' Jack's orneriness had spread around. Granddad went to town to look for a buyer. There he met a fellow by the name of Jim. He had heard about the absolute cantankerousness of Ol' Jack, so he bargained with Granddad: "Give me a job and I'll guarantee to make a first-class work mule out of that hybrid." Granddad hired Jim.

I suppose Jim had his good points, but for the life of me I could not make myself aware of them. He was brutal in his attitude toward animals. It soon became apparent, however, that Jim was the right man for Ol' Jack. Within a short time, Ol' Jack was a picture of docility, when Jim was around, at least.

After Jim moved on, Ol' Jack seemed to have a better disposition. Gradually Granddad and Ol' Jack became close friends. Ol' Jack turned into a plum good plow mule.

Still they had their little ups and downs. Perhaps Ol' Jack was just funning. He still enjoyed catching Granddad between the wall and the feed trough, pinning him there to beg the stubborn cuss to move. A mule tail, filled with cockleburrs, was an ever-present hazard, Ol' Jack did not even wiggle his ears as a warning.

When Granddad semi-retired, he occasionally lent Ol' Jack to neighbors, but in essence, Ol' Jack was semi-retired, too. When Granddad retired altogether, he retired Ol' Jack. He could have easily sold him for a goodly sum, but he allowed as how Ol' Jack had earned his retirement, too. After all, the two had developed a genuine feeling of affection. Ol' Jack, like fine wine, had mellowed some with the years, but, again like fine wine, he still had a kick.

Ol' Jack enjoyed more than four years of full retirement in his beloved pasture. He died at the ripe old mule age of 29½ years.

Even at the very end, Ol' Jack got the last laugh. I can almost divine his last thoughts of devilment as he became aware that it was his time: "Now, if I just lie down right here on the open grass and die, they'd have an awfully easy time hauling me out. On the other hand, that nice crop of crowded tree stumps there—they'd have a dickens of a time...." ❖

The Barns I Remember

By Emma Lewis

Barns with haylofts have gone the way of houses with attics. For those who played in either one, they hold remembrances of special playgrounds, replete with magic and make-believe. But while an attic was only a once-in-a-while place to play, a hayloft filled with loose hay was a fragrant retreat, good for all summer long.

There is no room in the modern barn for loose hay. All of it is baled into neat, tightly packaged bales before it leaves the field. These are then stacked in neat, concise rows in a neat, concise barn. Domino-stacked hay bales are efficient and space-saving, but they leave no room for children to crawl through, hide in or explore.

The barns of 60 or more years ago were different. The one I remember was built like a huge hovering hen, with an A-shaped roof and thick oak doors. The barn was made of wood, except for the nails which held

it together. It had a feedway, ample in size for a barn dance, cool in summer and warm in winter. The wide feedway was flanked by stalls for horses on one side and stanchions for cows on the other, with walkways leading to additional housing areas for growing calves and sheep. Huge bins in which corn and oats were held for immediate feeding lined the feedway.

In the middle of the feedway's ceiling was a rectangular opening to the hayloft. The loft was reached by a ladder that stood at about a 150-degree angle. It was steep but sturdy, securely nailed to a supporting rafter. Its steepness, however, never deterred my brother, sister and me from running up and down it whenever we wanted to.

On summer afternoons when friends came to play, the hayloft could be a stage for "show and tell" as well as a playground. The loft was the favorite place for the barn cats to bear their kittens. If you found them one day, you'd have to search for them the next, for the mother cat would have moved them to a better hiding place.

The mow did not extend over the calf and sheep sheds. Here on the roof rafters every year, dozens of barn swallows built their cup-shaped mud nests, safe from cats and children, but not all else. Sitting near the edge of the mow one late June afternoon, watching the graceful swallows catch flies and gnats to stuff the hungry mouths of their babes, we children were horrified to see a big black snake slithering its way noiselessly on a nearby barn sill, not far from the swallows' nest. My sister, Francie, started waving her arms and yelling. My brother Chris and I did likewise, but on the snake glided.

"You and Chris hurry down to the branch and fill your pockets with rocks," Francie shouted, waving her arms, "and anything for us to throw and scare it. But hurry! I'll stay here and watch it and try to frighten it away."

Chris and I hurried for the rocks and were back in no time with two dozen or more nice inch-and-a-half rocks, plus several sticks.

We threw all of them, but the distance was too great, more than 25 feet, and the sticks and stones all fell into the calf shed. The more we yelled and waved our arms, the more the snake kept flicking out its little red tongue.

"It's leaving! It's leaving!" Chris suddenly shouted, jumping up and down.

Sure enough, the snake was turning back on the side sill. We thought our yelling had done it. Little did we know then that snakes can't detect airborne sounds, but the birds were saved and we were glad. A few days later when we came

back, the baby birds were all gone. Had they flown away? Or had the snake returned?

In the hay, one dug tunnels and caves for hide-and-seek, and if we grew tired of this, there were always the barn sills to walk. The hay content in the barn loft was low enough now that the sills were exposed. The aim was to walk the entire length of the foot-square sill that ran the width of the mow. It was intercepted twice, however, by supports of the same size. To get around one of these supports, you had to hug the post with both arms and hook one foot around the other side until you could pull your body around it. If you fell off, you were caught by a bed of resilient hay and not hurt.

But the best barn adventure came in fall. Now the loft was almost full of hay after the summer's harvest. The little doors that closed the "hood"—the entry for the summer hay— hadn't been closed for winter yet, allowing ventilation to dry the new hay.

By climbing, tumbling and getting a face full of hay, one could reach the opening. This was near the peak of the barn roof. Standing on hay and hanging onto the edge, one could see all down the valley. The trees along the river almost a mile away looked dwarfed. It was a breathtaking view. One felt far away and above the world.

"Putting up" the hay in midsummer was a rite, a ceremony in which the barn played the queen, the hovering mother, ready to receive, store and hold the rich nutrients of the sun, soil and rain for the animals she housed.

Prior to this, though, the timothy, clover and alfalfa hay had been cut with a mowing knife. This was a 4-foot-long, wicked-looking metal affair equipped with 3-inch triangular teeth, honed razor sharp. The teeth worked back and forth on a cutting sheath. Woe to the small animal of the field—quail, pheasant or rabbit—which did not want to leave its young or nest unprotected, or thought that it could lie low and the clicking, cutting knife would pass over. Not so, for the knife cut low and the bird or rabbit might get its head or its legs mowed off. Almost every summer during my growing-up years, some baby rabbits or young birds were rescued and raised by my brother, sister and me—young animals made orphans by the mowing knife.

Once the hay was cut, it was raked into windrows to dry, turned once and stacked into small mounds for the hay wagons to gather.

A wagonload of hay would drive to the front of the barn. An 18-inch, two-pronged steel hayfork dangled down the front of the barn at a safe distance from the wagon driver's head. It was held in place by a pulley and an inch-thick hemp rope. A small rope swayed in reach of the driver's hand. When the wagon was in place, the driver would grasp the small rope and cautiously pull the fork toward him. When it was in reach, he'd grasp its hump and push with all of his strength, forcing it into the hay, being careful to adjust it so that it would pick up a maximum load. He secured the adjustable tines, picked up the small trip rope and moved to the other end of the wagon.

"All right!" he'd yell, and the man at the rear of the barn, driving the "pull-up" horse, would start it moving. As the horse started forward and moved out, the big hay rope running down the back of the barn through pulleys became taut and the hay began its ascent up the barn's front toward the entryway to the mow. Just as it entered the barn loft, it clicked onto a steel track and moved easily on the slide to the desired place.

"Whoa!" yelled the stacker in the haymow, as the forkful of hay reached the spot he wanted it to be, and in the same breath he'd yell "Trip 'er!" to the wagon man. The rope at the rear of the barn slackened, the trip rope jerked, and the bundle of hay fell into place.

The man and horse at the rear of the barn turned around to begin the trip over again. The driver set the hayfork, and forkful after forkful and load after load was put into the barn's loft.

"Stay away from the barn where the men are working," we children had been told by our parents. "You'll get in the way or you'll be hurt."

"Stay away from the barn where the men are working," we children had been told by our parents. "You'll get in the way or you'll be hurt." This, however, did not prevent us from climbing onto the garden gate that adjoined the barnyard. Here we had a good view, front and back, of the day's moving proceedings—the big wagons stacked with the new hay, pulled by two sturdy horses stepping in unison to the driver's commands; the seemingly magical ascent of the big bales of hay up the barn's front; the men giving each other orders with crisp, fast responses; the squeaking wooden pulleys as the ropes went through. It all held us fascinated. To our young and untried imaginations, it was a little like going to the circus.

Nothing is forever, though. The years have gone by and the time is past for the barns I knew and their attending activities. Some are still in use, including the one I remember, but their interiors have all been modernized. Others have been torn down to make way for progress and some have just been abandoned but left standing, their sagging ruins a mute reminder of the life and importance they once held.

Maybe, though, there is more than just memories of the old barns. Recently a friend persuaded me to go antique hunting with her. The item she wanted wasn't on display, so the proprietor took us to a room where he keeps big, "unpolished," cumbersome pieces. My eyes opened wide! What I saw and the prices they commanded would have made the old queens proud of their "treasures": wagon wheels, spring wagon seats, singletrees, jugs, milk cans, horse collars, even old frame timbers. My mind leaped. Did they have any of those two-pronged, steel-jawed hayforks?

I didn't see one and began to wonder what had happened to the one I knew. Does its owner tell fanciful tales of make-believe to those who will listen, of its being an instrument of torture of long ago? Or does he tell it like it really was, that it's just an old innocent but efficient hay clutcher which met its Waterloo with the advent of the hay baler? ❖

Moving a Farm: 10 Days to Travel 95 Miles

By John Fialkowski

In 1938 road conditions were not what they are today. When my parents bought a farm near Hamburg, Mich., some 95 miles away, we had to move the whole farm across those roads. I was 16 years old at the time when we loaded our hay wagon with hay, grain, blankets, tarps and other necessary things to make one trip. The next morning, we hitched the horses and tied eight milk cows to the wagon.

Following Dad's map, Chester, my 19-year-old brother, and I moved out. Mom had packed lots of food and a milk can full of water. The rest of the family was moving our furniture, farm machinery, chickens and pigs and anything else that could not walk. It took Dad about a week to move all our stuff. It made a long day to load the 1929 Chevy truck, drive 95 miles at 25–30 mph, unload and make the return trip.

With the wagon team and cows, it took Chester and me about 10 days to get to our new farm. Each day at noon we would pull into a farmyard to get permission to rest and water the cows and horses. The farm wives always would bring out cold tea or milk for Chester and me to have with our lunch.

In the evening we would pull into another yard to see if we could spend the night in the farmer's barnyard. We would milk the cows that evening and the next morning. We would give the milk to the farmer for letting us stay there. Every night we would be invited to have dinner with them and breakfast next morning. Chester and I were total strangers along that route and yet not a single farmer turned us away.

I don't remember just when Prohibition was repealed, but the house we moved into must have been a speakeasy. The house had a wing added on, which was a dance hall. A small bandstand had a sign over it reading "The Silver Slipper." The walls had bouquets of flowers and cupids painted on them. Besides the dance hall, there were six bedrooms, three big living-type rooms, a kitchen and a good-sized enclosed porch. There was a bathroom inside and two outhouses in back. Outside there were two big barns, a silo, a chicken coop, a pig shed and a cottage house.

That fall our well went dry. When we opened the covering boards, we found a hand-dug well lined with brick. It was about 4 feet in diameter and 15 feet deep. The brick wall tumbled down with a lot of dirt. Dad set up a pulley block with a bucket on a rope and had me go down with a small shovel to clean it out. In all that rubble I found a $2.50 gold coin, minted in 1914. I still have the coin.

I have many good memories of my life in Michigan around Hamburg and Whitmore Lake—fishing, swimming, free movies during summer, the roller rink over the water, cutting and hauling ice in winter and many more. Then the war came and we went....❖

A Toad for Every Cellar

By Mary Lee Reisch Moles

Eons before we were led to believe we would have a "car in every garage" and a "chicken in every pot," it was common knowledge that there was to be a toad in every well-organized cellar. This was certainly the case on our farm in southern Iowa.

We lived on a sizeable cattle farm, and our cellar had to accommodate winter provisions for family, hired hands and "poor relations" who lived in two of my grandfather's three tenant houses.

The old cellar, next to a smokehouse that was filled to the rafters with smoked hams, did its part each year to retain, precious and edible, the oncoming winter's provisions.

Of paramount interest to my childish existence was the fact that the cellar was home base of my good friend, Mr. Toad. The cellar was our only refrigerator, and I always accompanied Mother to it just before mealtime, where she obtained the milk, cream, butter, smearcase, kraut, etc., for the sumptuous meal to follow.

It was then that I could search for Mr. Toad, as I knew he would be hiding from me behind a crock of milk, keg of kraut or in one of his many elusive hideaways. I liked the feeling that this amphibian had been waiting for me to play the game, just as I had looked forward to seeing him.

One day when Mother became cognizant of my continued curiosity, after I once more asked her how long my friend had lived in this pocket-sized Carlsbad (or words to that effect), she decided that at 5 years of age, I was old enough to hear the truth!

Farm wives are always in a rush, but I shall long remember Mother taking the time to sit on a bench, blot perspiration with the corner of her huge ruffled apron, and take a long deep breath. Then, in the cool, cool cave with its gorgeous intermingling aromas, she explained that toads play an important part in keeping cellars free from bugs, flies, and ants.

She thought this particular Mr. Toad had been there a long time, but he and his cousins all had a strong family resemblance. Then Mother said, "Each time I see your little Mr. Toad, I feel I should apologize to him once again, at least in my thoughts." My expression induced her to continue, telling me that when she married my father, the engineer from the big city, he never had known the privileges of enjoying rural masterpieces produced by herds of Jersey cows. Each afternoon, Daddy would forsake his recently inherited, unfamiliar farm tasks for a sly trip to the cellar. There he would pick up a large, heavy crock of milk and have a long, cool drink. In the shadow of the cellar, little did he realize the telltale impression this left on the thick yellow cream which was in no way to be removed.

Each day when Mother made the journey for the supper provisions and saw the "break" in the cream, she believed Mr. Toad had been the guilty one, so she carried the remainder to the livestock troughs. Mr. Toad looked innocent enough, but who else could have done this? Dawn arrived, as it always does! When approached with the incident, Daddy readily admitted his imbibing in this matinee Lucullan delight.

Mother is 94 now. If I detect an occasional smile while she takes her afternoon nap, I just wonder if she is still endeavoring to figure how much of the precious dairy products she poured into the troughs for the livestock. Or, what happened to Mr. Toad? I think her smile is just a reflection of the fact that she thought Daddy was pretty clever to get away with it for so long, without Mr. Toad squealing on him.

What would a cellar be without a Mr. Toad? ❖

Pa's Diary

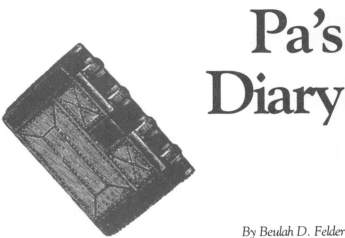

By Beulah D. Felder

I laid off rows all day. Cotton rows in forenoon and corn in afternoon. Weather fair and mild."

This is an excerpt from one of my most treasured possessions—a diary kept by my father, the late Thomas E. Dukes. The date of the entry is Friday, March 21, 1884. It matters not that that was before I was born, for the things recorded in this booklet are representative of what I remember of my father and my precious 15 years of living with him. I was the last of his and my mother's 11 children and I came to them in the mature period of my father's life. My mother was nine years his junior.

I see him stepping briskly down that furrow, his strong hands gripping a plow handle, guiding the plow as a horse or pair of horses pulled it, leaving behind a long, narrow groove with a low bank of loosened earth on each side. My father couldn't stand the cantankerousness of a mule and so his farming power was supplied by sleek, fat horses who were trained to pull a heavy load, but nevertheless were pampered.

Pa was happy that March morning, I have no doubt. Another spring was being born and it told in the redolence of fresh-turned earth, in budding trees and the flocks of robins that had returned. And there was hope in his heart—a hope that was and is always a farmer's—that this year would be better than last year.

He was doing what he liked. I recall hearing him say in his later years, "Some of my happiest days have been spent behind the plow." Farming was more than a method of earning support. At work in his fields with God as his partner or walking in his lovely woodlands, he found self-renewal—an essential to one of his idyllic nature.

April 16: "Replanting corn all day, the stand being very bad on account of larks having pulled it up." Those birds seem to have eaten a big share of the sprouting grain, for on May 1 is: "Finished planting rice and planted some corn which had been destroyed by the larks."

Rice, planted on lowlands, was a pretty, low-growing crop. Other grains grown were corn, oats, rye, peas and sometimes wheat. Cotton was his main money crop, but there was no stinting of acreage for foodstuffs. Animals as well as people must be well-fed.

Always we had our peanut patch, and there was an abundance of watermelons and cantaloupes, a large vegetable garden, sweet potatoes, sugar cane for making syrup and a spacious, fenced-in orchard.

Sept. 1: "Picking cotton." Cotton-picking began in August. My next older sister and I awaited the first day impatiently, and two of our cousins who lived in town would come out and stay with us so that they could share the good times. We knew we'd earn a little money, but that was secondary to the fun of gathering the white fleece from brown burrs that the sun had popped open, stuffing it in our knapsacks, then dumping it on a cotton sheet at the weighing-up place, talking and laughing as we "worked" and knowing that a lunch we had placed in the shade awaited us; not a midday lunch but a midmorning one, for we left the field when the sun got hot, then returned in late afternoon.

My sister and I did well if our enthusiasm for picking cotton lasted beyond two weeks, but other interesting events awaited us. High on the list were sugar cane grinding and syrup making. School was in session then and we begrudged time spent in the schoolroom, but there were the after-school hours that extended into night.

We stood around, watching the operation and filling ourselves with sweet juice from the ribbon-striped cane. A horse hitched to a long, stout pole that was slightly curved at one end went 'round and 'round in a large circle, making huge metal cylinders turn and squeeze juice from the cane as one of the men fed stalks of it into the squeezers. As the juice was extracted, it trickled into a barrel covered with a cloth which strained out the impurities. From this barrel the juice was transferred to a container beside an end of the evaporator, or cooker, from where a small stream of it poured into the cooker. As it traveled up and down channels, heated by a furnace fire beneath, water evaporated from it, and when it reached the far end of the evaporator, it came out a delicious, light-colored syrup that resembled maple syrup. There were gallons and gallons of it—enough for the family and for the families of the men on the place, who worked for my father, and their families.

At sundown came weighing-up time and the excitement of learning how many pounds we had picked. The pickers assembled and tied their sheets of cotton into bundles to be weighed by my father with huge scales that hung from a support between two upright posts. A stout hook attached to the scales held the sheet of cotton. As each person's cotton was weighed the name was announced, and my father would call out the number of pounds to his or her credit, then make a record of it in his record book. At the end of the week, the numbers were added and each person was paid.

As fast as the sheets were weighed, they were loaded into a waiting wagon to be taken to the cotton house in our barnyard. The last fun of the day for us children was a ride home, sitting high up on those soft bundles.

Nov. 19: "Cutting firewood." In the dining room on a wintry morning, the fire burned brightly as we sat down to breakfast. A typical early morning meal close upon butchering day was pork sausage and liver pudding, a bowl of hominy made from corn grown on our farm and a mound of hot biscuits.

At night we sat before a glowing fire in the living room or in my parents' room that sometimes substituted for the living room. I loved it all. The closeness of it bound the family together as a unit. There was interesting conversation and sometimes a game of Old Maid. My father had a keen sense of humor and he gave us some good laughs. Other times he spoke in a serious vein, offering us wise counsel. (I'm glad television had not been invented.) Then, as bedtime approached and the fire burned low, leaving a bed of glowing coals, he would ask that one of us bring him his Book.

It was the custom in those days for boys and girls to go home from school with a friend for a spend-the-night visit. A few years ago a gentleman who in his youth had had such visits with my brothers said, "When you went to Mr. Tom Dukes', you knelt down and prayed!"

So, my father read from the Book, often from Psalms: "Blessed is the man who walketh not in the counsel of the ungodly nor standeth in the way of sinners." After reading he would lead us in prayer. He implored we "live with an eye single to Thee and Thy glory."

On what is described as a cold day in January is recorded: "Butchered five head hogs which is the winding up of my winter killing." The usual number for the season was 18 or 20. At intervals a calf was butchered.

Feb. 6: "Hauled rails and made fence in afternoon." Ralph Waldo Emerson wrote, "There is a great deal of enchantment in a chestnut rail or picketed pine board." My father's rail fences were made from rails split from his pine trees, but I assume they held no less enchantment than Mr. Emerson's New England chestnut ones. Those fences stood proudly, too—no broken-down fences on my father's place—and there was beauty.

Our home was set in a big grove of long-leaf pines that looked over the heads of moss-draped oak trees. Beneath them grew wild-flowers and gooseberries.

We didn't have much money when we were growing up in those lovely surroundings, but we weren't money-conscious. I think we'd have been happier with more of it; yet would a store-bought toy have given us more pleasure than converting maypops into animals or chickens? Or constructing a wagon out of scraps of boards? We learned self-reliance on that farm.

And what could rival the joy of scaling an apple tree and picking a golden apple? Or climbing the grape arbor and plucking clumps of yellowish-green scuppernongs? Of course there was always the fear of meeting with a black snake, but that made it an adventure.

Or fishing in a stream that ran through a wooded section of pasture? Not a polluted stream, but one that was so clear in the shallow place where we waded and where the cows and pigs quenched their thirst that we could see white sand on the bottom.

All this wealth of happiness would not have been ours without the knowledge that a protecting love surrounded us.

My father was a man of strong physique and great courage, but he wept when the love of his life had been taken from him and he was left to live seven lonely years without her.

Would a store-bought toy have given us more pleasure than converting maypops into animals or chickens?

That same love extended to his children. I shall never forget a certain Sunday afternoon not long after my mother died. A family member found me alone, weeping. My father sent for me. I was no more than 8 years old. He lifted me to his knee and held me there, speaking comforting words, then reached into his pocket and placed in my hand a shiny half-dollar.

Those happy years with Pa ended suddenly seven years later on another Sunday morning. Soon after his death I learned that he had bequeathed to me a modest heritage, but his most cherished legacy to me is a collection of memories—memories that have helped me place the right value on certain things like truthfulness and honesty; memories that, through the years, have brought me joy and, occasionally, a tear. ❖

Farm Facts of Life

By Hazel J. Matthews

Living on a farm has its advantages in so many ways. Children learn the facts of life, being around animals and helping to take care of them. However, a small child, not being able to comprehend may be led to take matters into his own hands. Such was the case with my youngest brother and me. I was 7 and he was 4.

One of the milk cows showed up one morning with a beautiful little calf. We were entranced and spent practically the whole day atop the cow pen fence, just out of the reach of old Bess who kept a watchful eye on us.

The question before the house was, "Where did she get that calf?" Over and over, we discussed the possibilities. The best solution we could come up with was, "She stole it!" Another thing that puzzled us was that the adults in the family, who professed to know everything else, didn't seem to be disturbed—they just looked mysterious.

We had only one hope left. When Bud, the hired man, came in from work, he would tell us. He always answered our questions.

We were still atop the fence at sundown when he came up. "It's a purty little critter, ain't it?" was his grinning comment.

"Where did she get it?" we blurted out before he could gather his wits. We looked him straight in the eye without blinking, which seemed to disconcert him no end. He studied a minute, took a chew of tobacco and propped his foot up on the fence. We held our breath, our eyes never moving from his face.

"You all don't know where she got it?" he asked in astonishment. "Sure, she found it behind a hollow log down in the creek swamp."

We were so shocked at his answer that we almost toppled off the fence. It didn't sound exactly right, but Bud had always told us the truth, and we believed implicitly whatever he told us, so the matter was settled.

We went into conference and came up with what we thought a forthright solution. If Bess could find a calf behind a hollow log—she being only a cow—why couldn't we do the same thing? There lay the swamp, but it was getting dark, so we would have to wait until morning. Somehow we felt our decision would not meet with approval, so we decided to remain quiet. Children often have this uncanny sense of when to talk and when to remain silent.

Early the following morning after breakfast, when all the adults were occupied, we slipped out behind the barns and into the swamp, excited over the prospects of the calf we would bring back. We pictured the surprise of everyone and wondered how the grownups could have been so stupid not to think of our plan first.

As we went further into the swamp, following the trails, we recalled that in the past we had not seen any hollow logs, but Bud said they were there. We walked and walked; still no hollow logs and no baby calf, and we found ourselves coming back to the place we started.

About that time, we heard Mama's frantic calls. She had just missed us. We must have looked very disillusioned as we came into view. Knowing something was not right, she finally dragged the truth from us. No hollow log, no baby calf, no nothing.

She had a difficult time keeping a straight face; however, our expedition brought results, for not long after that we received an elementary lesson concerning the birds and the bees. We were cautioned that such things were not discussed in polite society. This left us with another question. "Why?" That one we were left to ponder over for a while. ✤

Bees A-Swarming

By R.J. Fowler

*B*ees a-swarming! Bees a-swarming!" Many's the time I heard my younger brothers and sisters yelling that announcement as loud as they could as they raced barefoot through the garden from the cherry orchard.

The beehives were kept in the cherry orchard because Mother said that was the best place for them. She said it assured a bountiful cherry crop. In this respect she was right, as I remember boughs so heavily laden with large, juicy, grapelike Black Republicans that they would not sway with the light early summer breezes. Keeping the bees in the cherry orchard also prevented them from having close contact with the horses and cows in the barnyard.

"Bees a-swarming! Bees a-swarming!" Back in the early 1900s, beekeeping on the farms of the Willamette Valley was a task for the farmers' wives and children. Usually there were only three or four hives, and some women found it difficult to obtain permission from their husbands to keep bees.

It seems bees and the man of the farm never did get along very well. (In later years, I learned that farm men had problems working with bees because of the odor of horses. Bees seem to detest strong odors and that of horses seems to arouse their ire the worst.)

I remember seeing my father come in contact with the bees on numerous occasions. First he would wave one hand around, trying to slap the offensive bee. Then the first bee would be joined by another. This caused Father to take off his hat and wave it. By now other bees would have come to the assistance of their battling brothers and sisters.

Father, with hat in one hand, was flailing the air with both arms by now, trying to ward off his attacking insect enemies. As he rushed off, waving his arms, he resembled a Dutch windmill running under full power of a wind off the Zuider Zee. He finally made his escape into some seedling fruit trees growing by the chicken lot close by the cherry orchards.

"Bees a-swarming! Bees a-swarming!" This call always caused a great deal of activity at our house. In fact, an outside observer might have said "Bees a-swarming!" created bedlam. The three younger children would each grab a milk pan and a spoon. Beating the pans with their spoons, the trio produced almost enough noise for a first-class charivari. But Mother had said that plenty of noise made it impossible for the worker bees to hear the buzz of the queen's wings. Not hearing her wings, they would settle on a tree or shrub.

"Bees a-swarming! Bees a-swarming!" This was always my cue to rush into the house for the water bucket and dipper. Usually the bucket was nearly empty, so I'd run pell-mell to the well to draw up a full bucket. In my haste, I'd spill some, but with the pail three-quarters full I would proceed to where the swarming bees were thickest in the air. Then, with the dipper, water was thrown into the air and onto the swarming bees. According to Mother, this was another sure way of causing bees to cluster, as the falling water was supposed to make them think it was raining.

"Bees a-swarming! Bees a-swarming!" On hearing this news, Mother immediately started searching for her long-sleeved blouse, old wide-brim straw hat, and a pair of her old gloves. She could never remember just where her beehiving things had been put after the last swarm had been hived. There was always a short but frantic search.

None of the things Mother used when working with the bees was store-bought. The loose-fitting blouse was made from a piece of seersucker. The old hat was one of the wide-brimmed garden type with white mosquito netting sewn around the brim. The netting hung down from the brim about 18 inches and was gathered around the neck with a drawstring. The gloves were women's dress kid, and even though they were leather, they were so thin the bees could and did sting through them.

"Bees a-swarming! Bees a-swarming!" After Mother located her special apparel, she would proceed to prepare a hive. The hive was never store-bought, either. It was always either an empty wooden soda box or soapbox, free for the asking from the storekeeper at Powell Valley. Until repainted, our beehives always had either "Three Star Soap" or "Arm and Hammer Soda" labels on them.

A bee entrance 2 inches by a half-inch was cut in the box end before putting on the new bottom. The new bottom extended out from the entrance 3 or 4 inches so as to make a landing board for the bees.

No fixtures of any kind were put in the box hive, although Mother would sometimes wipe the inside of the box with a cloth dampened with honey dissolved in water. She 'lowed as the odor of honey made the bees think it was their home and thus they would stay. Years later I realized they did not leave the soapboxes treated with honey because the odor of the soap was eliminated.

Once the swarm was put in the hive box, they were on their own—and in this respect they went to town. Since there were no frames, brood comb was built in the box crosswise or any way the bees desired, as I was to learn years later when examining some of the old boxes.

"Bees a-swarming! Bees a-swarming!" Mother had two ways of putting bees in her hive boxes. If the swarm clustered a few feet off the ground, she would take the bottom board off the box, shake all the bees into the box, turn the box over on the bottom board and leave them until dark. After dark, when all the bees were in the hive box, they would be moved to a permanent location.

If they were quite close to the ground, Mother would spread out a white piece of cloth under the bees or right next to them if they were so low on a shrub as to be on the ground. Again, she would shake or scrape the bees onto the cloth in front of the hive. Mother would then drum on the box with a small stick which she 'lowed caused the bees to think it was raining; also, they could not hear the queen buzz. Anyway, shortly all the bees would start moving to the hive entrance, slowly, steadily and stiff-legged.

After a few days a store-bought super would be put on the new hive. Preparing the new super was quite an event at our home. First there was the excitement of unwrapping the package when it arrived from Sears & Roebuck. Then there was the nice, clean odor of the basswood, pine and cedar.

I can see Pa yet, beating the air with his hat in one hand and trying to hold the mares down by the reins with the other hand.

The pieces making up the super and frames were all laid out on the kitchen table in the evening after dinner. Each of us youngsters got part of the super to put together while Mother nailed the sides and ends. The 24 one-pound frames were put into shape by folding the pieces into little squares. My, how nice and clean the little white frames were! We used to think how nice it would be when later in the year they were filled with new, white comb and honey.

To put the super on the box hive, Mother bored three 1-inch holes about 3 inches apart in the top of the box. Over the three holes she fastened a strip of metal queen excluder. She then set the super on the box and placed a lid on the super.

"Bees a-swarming! Bees a-swarming!" As previously mentioned, the menfolk on the farms did not get along with bees. It was that way at our place—Pa and the mares did not mix with bees.

I remember one time in April when Pa was hauling manure into a field he was preparing for kale planting. Pa had just entered the field with a spreader load when all of a sudden (as he said later) he and the mares and the spreader were surrounded by bees. Now it seems laughable, but then, to Pa, it was very serious.

I can see Pa yet, beating the air with his hat in one hand and trying to hold the mares down by the reins with the other hand. The mares were bucking and kicking and trying to run away. By then Pa had lost his hat, so he was holding the reins with both hands.

Since the thing to do was to let the mares run to get away from the bees, he let them go—and did they run. In fact, to Pa's way of thinking, they were going too fast, so to help slow them down he steered them to a plowed field and, at the same time, put the spreader in gear.

Well, as Pa said afterward, that load of manure was sure spread in nothing flat. Pa got the mares quieted down shortly and tied them to the fence at the other side of the field.

"Bees a-swarming! Bees a-swarming!" The bees with which Pa and the mares had clashed clustered on a low bough in the cherry orchard. Where they came from we never knew; they were not from any of our hives. Since they came from the direction of a small wooded area about half a mile away, we assumed they were wild bees.

By the time Pa tied the mares to the fence and reached the house, Mother had the swarm in one of her hive boxes. She "lowed it was one of the largest swarms she had ever seen—she believed there were at least five gallons of bees.

When Pa got to the house, he was still quite shaken by his experience with the bees. The first thing he said was, "Mother, the bees will have to go; get rid of them right away—today!"

Mother, of course, protested. Why give

the haying on the day after the holiday. On his return with the Model-T touring car, he ran into a swarm of bees. I was in the yard when Pa came stomping through the front-yard gate. He said to me, "Where is your mother?'

"In the house," I replied. From the way Pa looked and the way he walked, I knew something was wrong. So I followed him into the house.

His first words to Mother, as he took off his old straw hat and wiped the perspiration from his forehead, were, "Your bees will have to go!"

Mother asked, "Now what has happened?"

Pa said, "It was like this. As I was returning from Griffin's, a swarm of your bees tried to get into the Ford with me."

Mother asked, "Where is the Ford?"

"It is up the road a ways in the ditch because I could not fight bees and drive at the same time," Pa answered.

Then Mother said, "The bees you met were not ours because they didn't swarm, as the children have been watching them. So, I won't get rid of the bees."

I was then told to run up the road and see if the bees had clustered near the Ford. Upon arriving, I found the car in the ditch with one bow broken where it had come in contact with a limb of an apple tree which hung over the fence. Up in a back corner of the top of the car the bees had settled. As quickly as possible, I conveyed my findings to Mother and soon we had the swarm in one of her ever-ready soapbox hives. ✤

"Bees a-swarming! Bees a-swarming!" This call always caused a great deal of activity at our house. In fact, an outside observer might have said "Bees a-swarming!" created bedlam.

up all her lovely honey producers? Furthermore, the ones which had run into Pa and the mares were wild bees and Pa could have a problem even if we did not have any bees. Mother also "lowed that for a swarm of bees to come to you was good luck.

Pa snorted. "Only an old wives' tale. I haven't seen any good luck so far."

Mother said, "We have not had them long enough. Just give them a chance." With that, Mother headed for the kitchen.

When he heard Mother rattling the cast-iron hot water kettle on the kitchen range, Pa knew there was no use arguing further.

Pa had another confrontation with bees just before the Fourth of July. He had driven up the road a piece to ask a neighbor to help us with

Country Mud

By Gilbert C. Kettelkamp

nyone who grew up in a rural area in the early part of the present century will have little difficulty recalling what was meant by the expression "country mud."

In late winter and early spring the mud seemed to attach itself to everything that moved. It was carried into houses, schoolrooms and stores. It even went along into the churches on Sundays and was left there to become dried dirt to be cleaned up later in the week. It just seemed to be everywhere. There was only one hope—shared, no doubt, by both children and adults: summer would soon follow when the ground would again become hard and dry and mud could be forgotten for another year.

For winter, everyone had either a pair of rubber boots or overshoes to wear whenever he or she stepped out of doors, and that person had to clean that footwear and leave it on the porch before he could go indoors. However, in real cold weather, the mother might permit the child to bring the pair indoors and set them on newspapers behind the kitchen door. There they would be a bit warmer when they were to be used again.

In late winter and early spring the mud seemed to attach itself to everything that moved.

I grew up on a farm in south-central Illinois, near the small town of Nokomis. My life was no different from that of the other farm children who attended Gopher Hill School. Most of us wore overshoes in rainy or snowy weather. When we went inside we lined up our footwear along the wall near the door. We were expected to put it on again when we went out to play at noon or at recess. However, since the school yard was well covered with grass, we found it convenient to forget much of the time. A few of the boys wore rubber boots and just kept them on all day, but most parents and teachers did not approve of this practice. I am sure the reasons are obvious.

My fifth- and sixth-grade teacher, who was the son of our minister, usually walked the mile and a half to school each day. Whenever it was muddy, he shoved his house slippers into the tops of his boots. Then when he reached school, he took them out and wore them during the school day.

At that time there was also another kind of foot gear that was commonly worn on the farm. It was a combination felt-and-rubber boot. The inner part was made of felt nearly a half-inch thick, pressed into the shape of a boot high enough to reach up to the wearer's knees. Over the felt the wearer slipped a one- to three-buckle rubber shoe when he went outdoors.

Felt boots were extremely warm for outdoor wear. Indoors they were equally comfortable without the rubber covers. I can recall wearing the felt parts on cold winter nights when the family sat around the heating stove in the living room. The warm felt really cut off the cold drafts that always seemed to move along just above the floor. But customs change even with footwear. Felt boots seem to disappear around the time when World War I began.

Country mud was a great inconvenience on the farm. One had to wade through it to do the chores. One dragged his feet through it when he went hunting across plowed fields. It was also inconvenient when someone had to go to town to get the weekly necessities for the family. This 10-mile round trip was usually made on a Saturday. Of course on Sundays there was also the trip to church.

Roads in later winter or early spring became so bad that it was almost impossible to travel. The worst came when the temperatures were warm enough to thaw the upper level of frost in the ground, but not warm enough to thaw the frost at its extreme depth. The water could not soak into the deeper ground so it remained near

the surface where it mixed with the surface soil to make what we all knew was good country mud.

Roads in our community had once been graded with ditches along each side. But since there was no material available to give them a hard surface, water gradually collected in the middle where the horses and the steel wheels of the vehicles traveled. Gradually the horses' footsteps and the steel wheels cut deeper into the muddy mixture until at times the vehicles' axles dragged along on the muddy surface. When the conditions got that bad Father would put a heavy farm doubletree on even a light buggy so that the large horses could pull it through the deep mire.

I also traveled this road when I went to high school. One day as I rode horseback, my horse's chest dragged in the mud. The road was completely impassable, so the road commissioners closed it until it had dried out somewhat. I had to walk along back and forth to school on the grassy edge by the fence.

In my boyhood the deep mud provided some rather interesting experiences, some of which were not pleasant. I recall an incident that occurred on the road to our South Fork German Methodist Church. The road to the church wound around alongside the South Fork of the Sangamon River. As children, we regularly went to church for religious instruction on Saturday mornings during the weeks that preceded Easter. Those weeks were also usually the time when the roads were at their worst.

On this occasion my brother, my cousin and I started walking along the road to church. My brother and cousin, both several years older than I, were soon joined by another boy. As the four of us walked along the grassy strip next to the roadside fences, we were overtaken by the neighbor's hired man who was taking the family's two daughters to church in an old spring wagon. The vehicle had once been a surrey. Now the top and rear seat had been removed. The driver and the two girls all sat on the remaining seat at the front. On all four sides above the wagon bed there was board siding about 8 inches high.

As the wagon caught up with us, the driver stopped and invited us to get up into the back of the wagon. Of course, we were glad to accept. However, with no sitting space available, we had no choice but to stand and hold onto one another. Fred, our neighbor's boy, took a position holding onto the back of the seat. As smallest of the group, I was placed next in line with instructions to hold on tightly around Fred's waist. My brother lined up holding onto me with our cousin behind him; his heels were just inside the end gate of the wagon bed.

All went well until we started up the clay hill alongside the creek. On that slope the clay mud was at least 2 feet deep. As a result the horses had to strain in their harness to drag the heavy load forward. They gradually fell into an even step, their rhythm making the wagon surge back and forth.

I was holding tightly onto Fred, but as the horses' surge forward caught the four of us as our surge went backward, the pull on my arms was so strong that I could no longer keep my grip. My body fell backward against my brother; he fell back against our cousin. He had no place to go other than backward out of the wagon. He had scarcely hit the deep clay when my brother fell on top of him, forcing him deep into the mud. All the while, my brother had hung onto me. I was dragged down on top of the two others. By then, our cousin had lost his cap in the fall and was deeply buried beneath the two of us. Slowly we managed to untangle ourselves and take a look at the damage. The hysterical laughter from the occupants of the wagon gave us some idea of how we looked.

Since the weather was still rather cold, all of us were wearing heavy winter overcoats. The coats, our caps, our gloves and the rest of our clothing were all covered with muddy yellow clay. No one was hurt, but we instructed the more fortunate ones to give excuses for us to the pastor when they arrived.

We started walking slowly toward home on the grass alongside the fences. We were not in a particularly good mood, yet could not help laughing as we looked at one another. Our cousin was the worst. Not only were his clothes covered with mud, but his hair was a plastered mess.

When we arrived home, even our parents could not help but laugh at our appearance. But it was no laughing matter to us when we had to do a cleaning job not only on ourselves but on our clothes as well.

Country mud was something we learned to live with each year. We might not have liked it, but we tolerated it. Few of us would have believed that cement, blacktop, gravel and crushed rock would someday provide us with smooth, hard-surface roads over which we could ride comfortably at all times of the year. Ironically, there are now three large limestone quarries along that five-mile stretch of road to Nokomis from which rock is hauled and used for road surfaces for miles around.

Now as I think back to those boyhood days, there are recollections that have pleasant connotations. I can still see myself as I would come back to our house in the evenings after completing my part of the farm chores in the mud. My boots would be covered with the sticky stuff which I knew would have to be removed. Also, I knew there was one conven- ient and quick way for doing this. I could take an old broom in my left hand, grasp the pump handle and work it up and down. First I could scrub one boot in the runoff and then the other.

When the boots were clean enough, I could set them on the porch outside the kitchen door and go in to the kitchen for supper. After washing up I could join the rest of the family at the evening table and begin eating the warm food that Mother had prepared for the four of us. With warm food inside me, I knew it would not be long before I would forget all about the country mud that lay outside in the dark. ❖

Down on the Farm

By Agnes W. Thomas

Although I try to be an understanding grandmother, I seem to be losing my ability to understand today's youth. When I hear my teen-age grandson complain about not having anything to do, I feel the need to explain what children had to do when I was young. I don't know about city children, but I do know that life on the farm was work, work, work!

In the 1920s we 12 children lived with our parents on a farm in North Carolina. My father was a stern, hardworking man who saw to it that all of his children did their share of farm chores. I hated to work in the fields and often insisted that Mother needed me to help with the cooking and housework. Besides, I had a very fair complexion and, unlike young people today, I did not want a tan! But Father's word was law. When he said "Everybody get to the field!" that's what we did.

I hated to work in the fields and often insisted that Mother needed me to help with the cooking and housework.

From daybreak till dark we were in the fields every day except Sunday, unless it was too wet to plow or chop grass. How we children used to pray for rain!

You might think that a farmer's children would get lots of rest when the snows came, but not us. Before spring planting time, we had to get the seed peanuts shelled. I remember sitting around the roaring fire of our living-room fireplace. Each child held a pan of peanuts in his lap; a big basket for hulls was close by. My father did not believe in idle chatter; only the crackling of the fire and the popping of the peanuts broke the deep silence.

As we finished that task, Father found other jobs for us to do. There were new grounds to be cleared, fences or barns to be mended, or wood to be chopped. If he couldn't find anything outside to do, he would have us rake the yard, clean the stables or oil the buggy harness.

How we children hated to get up on those cold, dark mornings. The oldest boy was called first. It was his job to make fires in the fireplace and cookstove. On very cold days, he even had to make one around the water pump to melt the ice. By the time Mother had thawed the clabber (sour milk) to make biscuits, and fried the ham, we had fed all the animals and were ready for a hearty breakfast.

The older boys received very little schooling because they were needed at home. We girls and the younger boys were allowed to go most of the time. We walked three miles to attend a little two-room country school. The building was heated by a wood stove, and no one ever heard of air conditioning.

The first crop to be planted in the spring was tobacco. A large bed, usually about 12 by 20 feet, was prepared on the south side of the house. Then my father would sow seeds and cover the bed with a cheesecloth-like canvas. This was nailed down to the four logs which surrounded the bed.

Protected from the snow and frost, the little plants soon appeared. They were too thick to grow properly, so our job was to thin them out. I remember crawling along on a board which was placed from one log to another. With a spoon we carefully removed the excess plants along with any grass or weeds that might be growing among the tobacco plants.

Late in the spring the fields were plowed, harrowed, fertilized and laid off in straight rows. My father was very particular about having every row perfectly straight. He made them that way by using "laying-off" poles which were placed at intervals along the row. He would steer his mule and plow to the first pole, measure the proper distance to the next row, and place the pole there.

Next, the corn, peanuts and cotton were planted and the older boys were allowed to go to school for a while, but not for long. The warm spring rains made the seeds sprout

quickly—also the grass! Our dad couldn't stand to have one blade of grass mar his crops, so back to the fields we went to cut out grass and to replant any seeds that had failed to come up.

I don't know if our fields really needed all that hoeing, or whether our "slave driver" just wanted to keep us busy and out of trouble. We worked in the hot summer sun until early July when the crops were "laid by." We usually rested some in July, but the tobacco needed attention soon after the first of the month.

When the tobacco plants were about shoulder-high, we had to cut off the tops to prevent them from going to seed. This also forced the growth into the leaves. Next, the suckers had to be removed, and the worms! How we girls hated to touch those fat, green pests! Carrying a jar and a stick, we would rake the worms off the plants into the jar, then give them to our brothers to kill.

Working in tobacco was the most unpleasant task I ever had. The sticky juice clung to the hairs on my hands and arms, and that, along with perspiration and dirt, created a most miserable feeling.

About the time that school started in the fall, there was more tobacco work to be done. When its leaves started to turn yellow, it was time to begin the long curing process. A tobacco cart pulled by a mule or horse was driven down each row and filled with the ripe leaves. These were taken to the tobacco barn, tied in bunches with string, then looped upside down on oak sticks. The sticks were hung on tiers of rafters in the barn. Then a slow fire was kindled in a sort of fireplace in one corner. The smoke, drifting up through the tobacco, gave it a fine fragrance and a rich brown color. Someone had to sit at the barn all night to keep the fire at a smouldering stage and prevent the whole barn from going up in flames, which often happened.

After the curing process, the tobacco had to be graded—lugs, seconds, trash and good.

Then each pile was covered with an old quilt or canvas and kept for a few months. Next it was taken to a warehouse in the nearest town and sold to the highest bidder. If the tobacco brought a good price, it meant that all of us would get a new pair of shoes; if not, cardboard soles again!

In addition to the tobacco, there were other crops to be taken care of. I didn't mind harvesting the corn because it required less work. When ripe, the ears were broken off the stalk and stored in the barn to be used for feeding cattle and chickens. I didn't like pulling fodder because it was dry and brittle; bits of it always seemed to get under my clothes and make me itch.

The cotton required many hours of backbreaking work. By October, the "fields were white with harvest." We used big bags for picking cotton. With a strap over the shoulder, both hands were left

Polarine
THE PERFECT MOTOR OIL
CONSULT CHART

Your Tractor
Needs POLARINE

The engine of your tractor needs Polarine to protect it against heat and friction and dirt. Polarine maintains a cushion of oil between all moving surfaces—keeps them from getting too hot—prevents the dust and grit from grinding them away.

A tractor lubricated with Polarine works smoothly and willingly—whatever you give it to do it does well—for it runs on a cushion of oil.

Polarine keeps your tractor in service. A tractor laid up when you need it most is an expensive machine! It pays to keep your tractor running steadily — always on the job. It pays to use Polarine! That's why Polarine is used on farms everywhere in the Middle West. Every tractor needs Polarine—and a Polarine motor oil is made for every tractor. No matter what make of tractor you own, there is a grade of Polarine made especially for it.

Consult chart at any Standard Oil Service Station for the correct grade for your tractor.

Standard Oil Company, 910 So. Michigan Ave., Chicago, Illinois

free for picking. I remember wondering if God made the cotton boll in five segments because we had five fingers. The prongs on the boll were sharp and often scratched our hands. No such thing as a manicure for us!

We began picking cotton as soon as it was light enough to see, and when there'd been a heavy frost, our fingers were numb with cold. We built a fire at the end of the row to thaw out.

Digging peanuts was a dirty job. When the plants reached maturity, Father would plow them up and we children pulled the plants from the ground, shook the dirt off, then stacked them around poles to dry. After a few weeks a man with a picker was hired to come in and separate the vines from the nuts.

The peanuts were bagged for sale; the vines baled for cattle food. If we were fast, we children could pick up a bucket of peanuts from the ground before the hogs were let into the fields to eat the leavings. We enjoyed roasting peanuts, frying them in butter and sometimes we made peanut brittle.

Farming has changed quite a bit since I was young. With tractors and other modern machinery, it doesn't take as many people to harvest the crops, but I remember the "olden days" when everyone living on a farm had to work in the fields. I still like to go out to a farm and pick fresh vegetables, but I'm glad people don't have to work as hard as I did. However, the work didn't hurt me, and I believe today's youth would be much better off if all of them had more work and responsibility.

A person doesn't appreciate money if he's had plenty all his life; a youngster doesn't appreciate leisure time if he's never had to work. ❖

> *I believe today's youth would be much better off if all of them had more work and responsibility.*

Plowing Corn

By George King

When I see some of the great cornfields while driving in the Midwest, I think about how we raised corn on our farm in Camden County, Mo.

We had lived on the farm in the early 1920s, then moved to Linn Creek when my father became the rural mail carrier. We moved back to the farm and built a new home there when Bagnell Dam was built. The dam inundated Linn Creek in the early 1930s, forming Lake of the Ozarks. Everybody in the area had to move.

We had a farm of more than 160 acres, most of it ridges and hills used for grazing cattle. In the "holler," as we called the low ground,

We farmed these fields in a way considered primitive by today's standards. We started by breaking the ground with one-man plows.

we had four small fields marked by where the meandering creek, Possumfork, crossed them.

All of the fields put together made up about 40 acres of tillable land. One year in particular we had a great stand of corn in the 15-acre field just above our home.

We farmed these fields in a way considered primitive by today's standards. We started by breaking the ground with one-man plows, each pulled by a horse. Three of us worked the field using a singletree hitch, the singletree being a crossbar which attached to the harness in front and the plow in back.

After breaking the ground, we unhooked the plows and attached a triangular unit of heavy wood beams and steel spikes. We dragged the field with this tool, spikes down and the point of the triangle in front. We did this until the plowed clods of dirt were broken up into finer soil.

After that it was back to the plow, this time a plain, shovel-type plow, with which we could march up and down the field digging out little trenches. We made these as straight and evenly spaced as possible, and they became our corn rows. We planted seed corn manually, dropping a couple of seeds at a time about three feet apart in the rows. Others came behind us with hoes, pulled soil over the seeds and tamped it down firmly.

Our next step was watching the corn grow.

The weather that year favored us. We soon could see little shoots of corn coming up all over the field. Along with the corn we saw weeds. This called for more plowing and hoeing. We went back to the plain shovel plow and plowed between the rows to uproot whatever weeds were there. Some extra care had to be taken to keep from uprooting the new corn shoots and to keep the horse from eating them.

Men with hoes followed the plow to chop off weeds left within the corn rows and the stragglers that the plow might have missed between the rows. We stopped around lunchtime to sit and eat amongst some buck brush along the creek.

The corn flourished, growing thick and tall. But the season was not without incident.

Some of our hogs broke out of their pen and got into the lush green cornfield. It was early in the morning, still dark. We heard the commotion and knew what was happening. We had to get the hogs out of the field for two reasons.

In the first place, hogs raise havoc in a cornfield. They knock down and trample the stalks, waste the nubbins (small forming ears of corn), and tangle the stalks one with another.

We stopped around lunchtime to sit and eat amongst some buck brush along the creek.

Secondly, hogs can founder on fresh, green corn. They will eat enough to kill themselves if not stopped in time.

My father got into the field first, and I followed soon after him. We chased the hogs with a lot of shouting and hullabaloo and headed them out of the field.

In the midst of this activity I heard my father emit several colorful words. He had run headlong into a large wasp nest! They swarmed all over him, stinging him several times in the face. He began to swell badly after we drove the hogs out of the field. We weren't familiar with allergies in those days; fortunately he wasn't allergic to wasp stings. He applied some cool lotions to the stings and waited out the results. The stings made him mildly ill.

We saved the cornfield and had a good harvest. But the harvest meant even more manual labor. We cut the individual cornstalks at ground level with corn knives and stacked them in shocks, tied at the top. Later we went shock by shock and peeled off the ripened ears of corn, then fed the stalks to the livestock. We also fed the ripened corn to the livestock through the winter. ❖

A Valley to Remember

By J. Marshall Porter

For most everyone who attended and bought what the auctioneer was offering, it was just another farm sale. Farm women, some of them aging and toil-worn, were still seeking implements of toil such as churns, crocks, rakes, hoes, sewing machines and quilting frames. Genteel ladies were buying fine old glassware, handmade rugs and choice antiques to add to their luxurious surroundings.

Though a few were well-dressed, most of the farmers wore work-stained overalls and jackets of shiny leather or denim against the biting spring wind. Assorted hats and caps, mostly battered and worn, crowned the heads of these monarchs of the soil, and most of the locks their headgear covered showed a lot of gray.

The young grass that was trying to get started in the farmyard was being flattened by muddy, manure-stained rubber footwear. The owner of the farm was a small man. He was bent and gray and looked older than his 65 years. He followed the auctioneer and sale clerk closely, and looked fondly at each animal or implement that passed from his ownership to the highest bidder. He did not share the gay, noisy mood of the crowd of strangers who attended his sale. His countenance betrayed his feelings of finish and defeat.

The farmer's sale that day marked the end of an era—a way of life.

Neither could I share the crowd's mood of gaiety. From birth to late middle life I had lived in the valley, and we were neighbors of the Herb Flint family. His sale that day marked the end of an era—a way of life. It was the end of small farming operations in Flint Valley. One by one such sales had preceded the loss of another family who had ceased farming operations, and now Herb Flint was the last.

I had not attended the sale to buy anything, for I no longer had use for such items. I suspect I was there to try to relive, in memory, my

earlier life in that valley. Those small, irregular fields where we used to trade work with neighbors to harvest grain and hay were overgrown with briars and sedgegrass, and the vacant buildings and farmyard fences were falling to ruin. I began remembering the valley as it used to be.

Wars and rumors of wars and easier and higher-paid jobs had drafted or lured the young people away. As the owners grew too old to carry on, they had to lay down their burdens, and another farm in the valley that had nurtured staunch American families for a century and a half was left to go back to wilderness.

Herb Flint was a victim of "rumors of wars." Herb's son ran his sizeable dairy operation. Herb had rented an adjoining farm which he was clearing so as to have land enough to make the dairy profitable. Then his son was drafted into the military service with but two weeks' notice. He had to leave his young wife and a child, his aging parents and his partly harvested hay crop in mid-June.

Not with the help of the senator, county agent, Red Cross or Hardship Agency were they able to defer induction until after harvest. Nor could arrangements be made to find someone to help run the dairy until the son served his two years—and this in 1955, 10 years after World War II was over. The aging father was left to try to carry on alone. The rest of the summer and winter was all he could endure, and that day he was selling out.

Forty years ago I was growing up in that valley. It was teeming with action then. Plowmen could be heard from the hilly pasture fields and ewes bawled to call their straying lambs. Dinner bells rang at mealtime to bring families together at the tables.

Nearly a dozen farms gave us two weeks of following a steam-powered threshing machine from farm to farm, as we all helped each other thresh our grain crops. One could never forget the fine neighborliness of the farmers of the valley as they worked together. The womenfolk helped each other prepare bountiful dinners and suppers for the men. Getting together gave them a little social life.

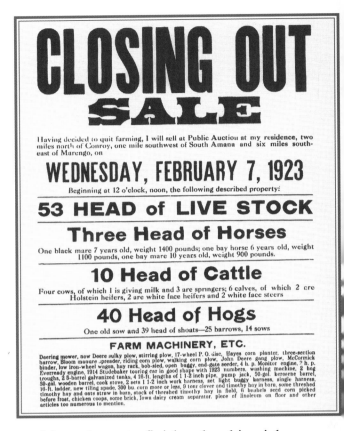

Many times, to finish a threshing job, we worked until we could see sparks flying from the smokestack of the steam engine, and from the grain stacks see the first lightning bugs in the coming darkness. Finally came the long, shrill blast from the steam whistle that told us we were finished with that neighbor's crop.

There was the orderly stampede at the old wooden pump to get water to wash up for supper, and what suppers they were. We were a hungry lot. We had worked from the noon meal until nearly 9 o'clock with only generous pieces of fruit or squash pie around midafternoon. We expected to work long days during threshing time, and no one grumbled about being overworked, even though such a day of working in grain dust often made your bones ache like a dose of flu when you tried to sleep that night.

Nor was threshing the only job which brought those neighbors working together. There was butchering, apple cutting, barn building, and quilting parties for the womenfolk during winters.

In fancy, I can still hear the chimes of sleigh bells breaking the silence of our valley on a cold, clear winter night. I hear the gay voices of our young people, my own among them, when we went on sleighing parties to dances, surprise parties and church socials. Every home in the valley was home to all of us, and I like to think again of the pleasures we enjoyed together.

Though the people of the valley were of mixed faiths, it could be said that we worked together, played together and prayed together. On Sundays the young folks walked down the dusty or muddy roads in a group and separated at the crossroads, each going to the church of his faith. We met after the services were over and walked home together, and got together again that afternoon at the ball ground or swimming pool. In winter we would skate on the pond, or coast from the snowy hillsides .

Our mothers were staunch believers in the healing power of prayer, and in cases of illness when the good mother was nearly worn out caring for a sick member of her family, a neighboring wife would come to her relief. They would pray together for the recovery of the patient and their prayers were respected and welcomed, regardless of the faith they practiced.

I am not trying to imply that our valley was a paradise in which the people were saints. Our people were human, and there were the little petty jealousies of families that managed better and seemed to have better luck than others. There were always the tales and jokes about those with stingy or peculiar little traits, but if ever a family was in need of help of any kind,

every neighbor would forget any differences and do his utmost to help in any way he could.

And then with 1917 came the World War I. The young men left the valley for jobs with higher pay, and the draft took most of the available young men because our farms were not considered big enough to merit deferments for men of draft age. Our young people in the valley began thinning out. Some of them are sleeping in France. None of the others ever came back to the farms to stay. One by one the owners got too old or died, and the farms were allowed to grow up with briars and brush. One would have had to live there to know where the fields used to be.

There was no great amount of farm products sold from the farms. Butter, eggs, fruit and vegetables were our main crops. The family food was raised and enough was sold to make the cash income, which was often pitifully small, but these families were self-sustaining and were never out competing for employment in the labor market.

There must be thousands of such desertions of farm communities in our country. From such communities came leaders, and statesmen— people of integrity who earned their bread by the sweat of their brows with a firm faith that, with God's help, they couldn't fail.

Life was simple then. We knew what it was to work from dawn to dusk and the blessedness of falling into a peaceful sleep with the night music of whippoorwills and katydids. ✤

Summertime Work & Play

The August sun seared its way into our lives again that day long ago. Another day without rain—oh, well, the crops were long since burned to a golden crisp in the brutal drought. Summer refused to give in to the steadily shortening days and the relentless onslaught of the season.

It was a brutal afternoon for a boy of 12. The breeze—even on the hilltop we called home—refused to blow. The creeks had been reduced to a few tepid waterholes barely able to accommodate hot tired feet. Even the shade of the huge oaks surrounding our farmhouse refused to give much comfort; the leaves seemed to be losing their lock on life already—two months before they should.

My pal Chester walked up through the heat, carrying his rifle and suggesting an afternoon hunt.

"Aw, it's too hot to hunt," I said. "Probably wouldn't see anything anyway."

"C'mon," Chet retorted, "I didn't walk 2 miles just to sit here and sweat. Besides, I know a place we can cool off."

That hope was enough to pull me away from the front yard and elicit permission from Mama. With my single-shot .22 under my arm I jawed at Chet as I reached the edge of the yard: "Well, what's keepin' ya?"

Chet was quickly in the lead. Over a couple of hills—and the dells between—we plodded. I had been right; neither rabbit nor squirrel rousted about in the heat. The only sound was the chirp of the cicada and the soft padding of our feet, wary for prey. Instead of directing us toward the third rise, Chet turned parallel to the slope and headed toward an outcropping of rocks. I knew of a cave spring which normally flowed from the base of these rocks; I also

knew the water long since had subsided with the drought of the summer, sinking to subterranean rocks.

"I found it last week," Chet said as we neared the cave. A farmer had dug out the mouth of the cave and had run piping back to what must have been a small reservoir. He had built a sizable holding box for the precious water; lowing of nearby cattle told me his work had not been in vain.

At first Chet and I dipped handfulls of the pure, cold spring water, then wetted handkerchiefs for faces and hot, dirty necks. Next we were sitting on the edge of the box, feet dangling frigidly inside as we talked. Dare led to double-dare and soon we were in the water—where we stayed until the icy water forced us out.

By the time we walked home, it was evening. I guess our body temperatures had dropped enough not to notice the heat. That night the breeze still wouldn't blow and the house was just as hot. Still, a friend's discovery had helped me make it through another August afternoon on one of the hot Good Old Days down on the farm.

—*Ken Tate*

The Summer Kitchen

By Pauline McClellan

When I was a youngster being raised on our dairy farm in western New York near Niagara Falls, our house on our 45-acre farm was a two-story, pre-Civil War building. Upstairs there were two very large bedrooms—one for us children and the other for Ma and Pa. It also had a large crib in it for our little brother Walter. Downstairs there was a front porch, living room, dining room and kitchen.

At the entrance to the kitchen from outside there was still another room which was only livable in the summertime. We called this room the summer kitchen.

The summer kitchen is where we cooked and ate during the summertime. The rest of the house was closed to us children during the daytime hours. It was only at night when we were getting ready for bed that we were allowed to pass through. Often we slept in the hayloft in the barn or camped out, and so it was days before we went into the main part of the house. Anna, our oldest sister, would have the house freshly wallpapered and house-cleaned, and she frowned on us children coming in. The house took a minimum of time to care for this way, leaving Anna free to do other jobs around the place.

One of these was canning fruits and vegetables for our winter food supply. This was, however, still done in the main kitchen where there was a large wood-burning stove and a large round kitchen table to work on.

The summer kitchen had at one time been a porch which had been enclosed by a former tenant. There was only one window and a screen door which let in the fresh air and sunshine. In the summer evenings, for some reason, the flies would sit on the outdoor side of the screen,

> **The summer kitchen is where we cooked and ate during the summertime. It was easier and cooler to light up the kerosene stove instead of the big wood-burner in the main kitchen.**

John Slobodnik

and Anna, trying to chase them away, would make paper strips from the newspapers and hang them over the door, and put balls of cotton balls on them, too.

Just before school closed each year, Anna would get the summer kitchen ready by painting it a cool lime green color. Then she would scrub the linoleum rug on her hands and knees. Next, she and Ma would move the large square table which had been pushed against one wall during the winter, and center it in the room. Anna had already been to the five-and-dime store where she had purchased a square of oilcloth covering for the table. Now, with the new oilcloth and clean organdy curtains in the window, the room looked shiny and cozy. An assortment of odd, unmatched chairs were placed around the table, and four wooden shelves on one wall, cleaned and covered with newspapers, were ready for the dishes, pans and silverware.

Next the portable kerosene cookstove was brought in. It consisted of two burners and stood on four metal legs, and had a glass jug of kerosene attached.

CAN MORE MEAT

USE *Ball* JARS FOR SAFETY AND ECONOMY

Safe and economical, yes—but more too—meats canned in Ball Jars are delicious to eat and easily and quickly served • Insist on Ball Jars Caps and Rubbers for your meat canning • They seal tight and stay sealed.

GLASS TOP SEAL for MASON JARS

Many women prefer the BALL Glass Top Seal Lid for meat canning. Simple, sure and easy to seal — this lid forms an all glass Mason jar.

Ball PERFECT MASON

Ball IDEAL

BOTH JARS MADE IN WIDE-MOUTH ROUND AND SQUARE

BALL BROTHERS COMPANY
MUNCIE, INDIANA

Send this Ad with your Name & Address

This is where we would cook most of our meals for the rest of the summer, and eat them. It was easier and cooler to light up the kerosene stove instead of the big wood-burner in the main kitchen. However, if there was any baking or chicken to be roasted in the oven, then the wood-burner was put to use.

Eggs on our farm were plentiful and when Ma was very busy, we children cooked many a light lunch of scrambled eggs on the oil stove. There was always a pot of fresh coffee in the kitchen, and we children would enjoy a cup of it also with the grown-ups. This was before coffee was frowned on as a beverage for children.

There was a small water pump in the corner, as there was a well underneath one corner of the summer kitchen. We had a ready supply of water on hand, although there still was a larger water pump out in the back yard. There was a small bench in one corner with a basin and bar of soap where we washed up before we ate.

Our cats, Katy and Tally, had their litters of kittens in a couple of cardboard boxes on the summer kitchen floor one summer, and I remember how the hired man, Kenny, laughed when he read my sister Jennie's note pinned over the boxes. It said "The Maternity Ward."

In the corner by the screen door was the old Maytag washing machine. Once a week Ma and Anna would pull it to the center of the summer kitchen, fill it with water and tackle the large pile of laundry. We had a small gasoline engine which only Pa could manage to start up, which he did by turning a big wheel, and the engine would start up with a *Putt-putt*. A belt ran from the engine to the washing machine, providing the power to run it. All day long Ma and Anna washed and rinsed the clothes, hanging them out on the lines in the back yard. How fresh and clean the clothes smelled as we brought them in later and folded them at the square table.

Ma wouldn't dream of washing clothes on any day except Monday, and early in the morning she would be busy at the task. I still remember the 101 Bleach she used, and the Gold Twins Soap Flakes.

Sometimes when she only had a "hand wash," or when Pa wasn't around to start the engine, the wash would be done in the large galvanized washtub (which we also used to bathe in), with the scrub board. She would use a yellow bar of Fels Naphtha soap, which did a very good job. Once, Mrs. Schul, our farm neighbor, made a batch of homemade laundry soap and gave us a few bars. This was very good, and the clothes came out clean and smelled really fresh.

To wash or hang up clothes on Sunday was absolutely forbidden by Ma. Though our house was far from the main highway, to have anyone passing by on Sunday to see the clothes on the lines was unheard of, so if there was any hand wash to be done, it had to be done any day except on a Sunday.

In 1938 we moved from our farm on the outskirts of the city to another farm further out on Lockport Road. Pa and my older brother Fred and a crew of Fred's friends Ma and Pa had hired tore down the house, large barn and other buildings and moved the lumber by truck to our new farm.

Today Fred and his wife Clara still live in the house which was built from the lumber from our old farmhouse and barn. ❖

The rest of the house was closed to us children during the daytime hours. The house took a minimum of time to care for this way, leaving Anna free to do other jobs around the place such as canning fruits and vegetables for our winter food supply.

An Apron Full of Memories

By Helen M. Sapp

This conversation opened a door in the attic of my mind, a door marked "Growing Up," and I became aware of how many of my childhood memories were tied to my mother's aprons.

During a recent and all-too-infrequent visit with my mother, I mentioned that if she wanted to know what to give me on the next gift-giving occasion, I would really like two or three homemade aprons. She looked surprised and was speechless for a few seconds before half-whispering, "Aprons? Homemade aprons? I didn't know you wore aprons!"

"Not all the time," I stammered.

"I thought you younger girls considered aprons old-fashioned. Why, I very seldom wear an apron any more," she said almost proudly.

This conversation opened a door in the attic of my mind, a door marked "Growing Up," and I became aware of how many of my childhood memories were tied to my mother's aprons. Most of all, I came to realize that aprons were more than just garments worn to protect clothing. They were symbols and they had the ability to convey unspoken messages from the wearer.

The aprons to which I refer weren't the flimsy, frilly kind. They were sturdy and serviceable, usually made of printed cotton, usually the pinafore style and nearly always handmade.

Anytime my mother was working in the kitchen, she wore an apron. When she went into the kitchen to begin fixing a meal, the apron was put on first. I can still hear her muttering, "And me in this old, dirty apron," after an unexpected caller had departed.

My mother's aprons said, "I am the person in charge here." They also said, "I work hard."

Aprons didn't always stay at home. Ladies sometimes took their newest or nicest aprons visiting, too. One was placed in the box or basket with cakes, pies and covered dishes that went to family reunions, family birthday and anniversary celebrations and holiday meals. They went to help in the kitchen at church suppers and to the sad occasions, such as after-funeral gatherings—any place women knew they would help prepare and serve food. If someone had forgotten her apron, she would borrow one from the hostess or fashion one from a dish towel. On all these occasions, an apron represented being part of the kitchen camaraderie.

Aprons would say, "I am here to work," when friends went to lend a helping hand at butchering time. The men usually did the outside work, killing and scraping or skinning the animals, while the women stayed in the kitchen, chatting and fixing the noon meal. After the meal was over, the dishes were done and the decks were cleared to begin cutting and processing the meat.

How well I remember aprons being brought to our house and worn through the two-day task of making fruit butters. During the first day, the aprons collected splatters of fruit juice while paper-lined washtubs collected pieces of apples, pears or peaches.

On the second day, the aprons took in the smell of smoke from the open fire while the kettle of fruit took its time cooking and the workers took turns manning the long-handled stirrer and returning to the house to bring out another sack of sugar.

When the work was finished the aprons were rolled up and tucked into paper bags with two or three jars of warm fruit butter. The workers then sat down to end their visit over coffee and a slice of bread topped with a sample of the day's handiwork.

I can still recall the speck of pride I felt when I was given one of Mother's aprons to wear while I helped prepare fruit or vegetables for canning, jelly or ketchup making. Back then and there, adults didn't discuss much with youngsters, but my borrowed apron said, "I'm important, too—well, sort of."

My mother's mother was a farm woman and she wore an apron all day unless there were visitors to sit and talk with in the sitting room. Then her apron was hung with her homemade sunbonnet on a hook on the kitchen wall.

One day when Mother and her sisters were young girls, Grandma was away from the farm and hadn't returned by milking time. Mother's oldest sister, Florence, decided to milk the cow. The cow was unaccustomed to being milked by anyone but Grandma and she refused to stand still. Undaunted, Florence went to the kitchen, disguised herself in Grandma's apron, returned to the barn and successfully milked the cow, probably one of the few times an apron told a lie.

Being a sentimental person, I have among my keepsakes three special aprons. One is a serviceable type which belonged to my dad's mother. Another is a pretty pink organdy number given to me years ago when I helped serve refreshments at a cousin's wedding reception. The third was my own very first apron, made for me by my Aunt Florence. It is printed with "Mary Had a Little Lamb" in words and pictures.

Today aprons are considered by most to be little more than novelties. There are barbecue aprons for men and women, aprons lettered with comments such as "Who invited all these tacky people?" or "I'd rather be playing tennis." Some are painted with designs to resemble tuxedos, or underwear or even less. There are cute frilly aprons and stylish sheik aprons, the kind we slip over a hostess outfit to arrange a tray of hors d'oeuvres and make sure our guests catch a glimpse of us.

The aprons of yesteryear are becoming scarce, probably gone the way of house dresses, but, Mom, I do still wear them. I wear one when I'm doing something messy, or when I'm in a domestic mood, and sometimes just because I'm feeling a little homesick and wishing you didn't live a thousand miles away. ❖

Barn Dances

By Dorothy Mikkelson

When I was a girl in my teens, growing up on a farm out near a small Midwestern town in the late '20s, barn dances were the favorite recreation of young people. Those farmers who had a large-enough barn to accommodate a sizeable crowd and a fairly good floor in the hayloft were the envy of their neighbors. A wooden staircase leading from the ground floor to the hayloft was the dubious means of getting to the top, and there was many an accident as the boards used for steps were often loose with nails protruding.

The farmer's children were usually given the not-so-easy job of sweeping and cleaning the loft of dirt and hay for the Saturday-night dance. Some form of powder or wax was used on the rough boards to make it a little easier for the dancers to move their feet, but after a couple hours of heavy traffic, they returned to their original shape. Many a lady's heel was broken on a nail or rough spot on the floor.

On each side of the loft were large openings through which the hay was forked to the mangers below. These openings posed a serious problem, as one could accidently fall through. Serious injury was not likely, however, as the mangers were usually full of soft hay.

Musicians at those affairs generally were men or ladies of the neighborhood who had a natural talent for music; very few had the opportunity for a formal education in music.

Musicians at those affairs generally were men or ladies of the neighborhood who had a natural talent for music; very few had the opportunity for a formal education in music. The orchestra was one or two fiddles, a guitar and mandolin and the old pump organ. The familiar dances then were the waltz, two-step, circle two-step, and the square dance which has come back into popularity today.

Transportation to the dances was by car, wagon, buggy or horseback, and many young boys thought nothing of walking for miles over the hills, then dancing all night before walking home again.

These dances were usually held during the summer months, as the barn would be too cold in winter. There were a few dances held in the living room of a neighbor's house. Occasionally an ambitious farmer would lay planks in the farmyard to accommodate dancers.

Lunch was usually served around midnight at the dance, and consisted of cakes, pies, sandwiches and hot coffee, brought by the ladies attending.

Lanterns were hung from the rafters of the barn. These burned kerosene or gas, as electricity had not reached that area yet. I never knew a barn to catch fire, but it seems a miracle none did, as there was many a fight started when the young men imbibed a little too heavy when the drinks were passed around below.

The small children slept on quilts on benches placed along the sides of the hayloft. Meanwhile, their parents danced the night through until the cock crowed below. The sun was often rising over the hill to the last call of "Do-se-do and around we go." ✤

Grandpa's Farm

By David B. Sabine

When we were children, my brother, sister and I had an unusual advantage. In the winter we lived in Yonkers, N.Y., a city of about 125,000 people with a school system reputed to be the best in the state. In the summer, we went to Grandpa's farm and lived a real rural life. "The Farm," near Boston, produced fresh fruits and vegetables, so we had the best of both city and country living.

The closest city was Brockton, the shoe city, about 10 miles away. The nearest neighbors lived in Brookville, about 2 miles distant, a village of a few houses, a church and a general store. The latter was like nothing we had ever seen and we were fascinated—a fascination that was fresh every year.

We usually traveled to the farm on the Fall River Line, but even the wonders of sleeping in bunks on these ships could not quiet our impatience. When we finally arrived, there was a grand rush to see what was new. There was a pair of buff-colored cats (called Tweedle Dum and Tweedle Dee because we couldn't tell them apart) and a new litter of kittens; in the barn there was our old friend Kitty, the horse, a couple of cows and frequently a new calf; in their hutches were baby rabbits in profusion; in the henhouse, Barred Rocks and Rhode Island Reds with their brand-new chicks; and, allowed the run of the yard, were a pair of guinea fowl and a bantam rooster.

In the summer, we went to Grandpa's farm and lived a real rural life. "The Farm," near Boston, produced fresh fruits and vegetables, so we had the best of both city and country living.

Running down the driveway to meet us was the dog—a Boston bull with one blue eye and one brown eye who, for some unknown reason, was named Fudge.

He was a trickster. In the evening Grandpa liked to sit in his rocking chair by the wood-burning cookstove and smoke his pipe. Fudge liked to sit there, too. When Grandpa got well settled, Fudge would suddenly rush to the window, looking to the front gate and

barking furiously. Grandpa would reluctantly get up to see who was coming. There would be no one there, so he would turn back to his chair, only to find Fudge comfortably ensconced there. Fudge got away with this maneuver night after night because Grandpa could never be sure that this time someone might be coming.

Although small by most any measure, "The Farm" offered us many adventures. There were woods all around us, but we weren't allowed to

On the road to Brockton, Grandpa had regular customers who looked forward to his strawberries, raspberries, fresh corn, eggs and so forth.

most New England homes, the parlor was used only on Sunday. To anybody else, it would be primitive. To us, it was heaven.

To get up early and do the chores with Grandpa before breakfast was a much-sought privilege. By the time we had helped him feed the horse, cows and chickens, milk the cows and carry the milk to the kitchen, we were ready for a gargantuan breakfast.

On the road to

go there without an adult. Grandma was always afraid we would get lost, and after a few harrowing and gruesome tales about what happens to children who get lost in the woods, we abided by her rules.

At the end of the road, past the entrance to the pasture, was a gate beyond which lived a mystery man. We had all sorts of ideas about him, and one day the thrill of adventure overcame our fears and we climbed over the gate.

He saw and called us. Trembling inside, we went, and he invited us into his house. You can imagine our surprise (and perhaps a little disappointment) when we discovered that he was just an ordinary man living alone and trying to wrest a living from his few rocky acres!

At home we had electric lights, gas stoves and steam heat; here there was no plumbing— only "back door" conveniences. The kitchen and dining room were lit by kerosene lamps which also served to light our way to bed and, like

Brockton, Grandpa had regular customers who looked forward to his strawberries, raspberries, fresh corn, eggs and so forth, so once or twice a week, depending on the amount of produce available and how well the hens were laying, he hitched Kitty to the democrat and drove off to see them. Only one of us could go with him, so there were many arguments about whose turn it was.

Like many small New England farms, Grandpa's was not thoughtfully laid out. The barn was on a rise slightly above the house and too close to the well, so the water had long been too polluted for human use.

Lugging water was another job we didn't mind. The spring was only about 200 yards from the house, and an invasion of the pasture when the cows were there offered all sorts of adventures. Moreover, we had to go down the wood road to the pasture gate—a popular trip. Occasionally, after a long dry spell, the flow slowed enough so that Grandma felt that the cows might get too close to the source and pollute the supply. Then we used another spring in a hay field.

This was a limestone spring with the coldest, sweetest water I ever tasted, but the flow was insufficient for constant use. Moreover, it was a good quarter-mile farther from the house, so lugging water from there was more of a chore. We carried water from the pasture in open buckets, but from this spring the spillage, due to the longer distance and rough walking, was too great, so we used milk cans with tight covers.

Frogs, of course, abounded in both springs. My brother and I used to catch them but were never able to keep them in the buckets. With covered milk cans, we saw our chance to get some home. We had plenty of pets but no frogs, so one day, while filling the cans at this spring, we caught a few and finally succeeded in getting at least one frog in each can. It is not hard to imagine the consternation when Mother and Grandma opened the cans. The frogs jumped all over the kitchen, the women screamed and we laughed hysterically—but not for long! We never quite understood why there was such a to-do over a few frogs, but we understood our punishment! Although Mother lived to be 97 and Grandma lived to be 95, I don't believe either one ever fully forgave us.

Time moved on, as it usually does, and we grew up. My brother graduated from Tufts University and I had just finished my first year there when Grandpa developed a terminal illness. I went to the farm and took charge under his direction. I was only a fairly skilled farmhand, but with Grandpa on hand, I got along all right. I milked the cow, gathered the eggs, hoed the corn, mowed the hay and collected the produce for market. I hitched Kitty to the democrat and drove the route to Brockton with Grandpa at my side. He and I became very close that summer. I discovered that he hadn't always been a farmer, but was a very interesting person who had led a fascinating and adventurous life.

There was never any question of my not returning to college. When fall came, Grandma sold the horse and cow and I split enough wood for a hard winter. Also, I went over every weekend to make sure they were all right. Then Grandpa died in November and Grandma sold the farm for the timber. My brother and I discussed buying it for a summer place because we loved it—the wood road, the pine grove where we chewed checkerberry leaves for their wintergreen flavor, the secret cave under the wisteria tree where we smoked cornsilk, the general store in Brookville—but there was no way we could raise the money.

When I went by there some 20 years later, I found it completely overgrown. A New England hurricane had removed both house and barn, and the Commonwealth of Massachusetts had turned the land into a bird sanctuary. ❖

We carried water from the pasture in open buckets, but from this spring the spillage, due to the longer distance and rough walking, was too great, so we used milk cans with tight covers.

The Price of Progress

By Virginia T. Joslin

Things were never the same at Grandma's after the advent of the Delco pump. I guess you might say that it was the installing of the electric system that started it all, but I wasn't aware of the fact that a new era was born until the coming of the pump.

Grandpa was the first farmer for miles around to install his own electric system—the Delco System it was called, and it was a proud occasion for Grandma the night she pushed the little pearl-tipped button in the wall and the frosted glass basin hanging from the ceiling flooded the dining room with bright, yellow-white light. We were all there—the whole family—smiling, proud, shining a little ourselves as we followed Grandma through the house and into each room and, one by one, she pressed the buttons until the whole house was lighted.

It was a proud occasion for Grandma the night she pushed the little pearl-tipped button in the wall and the frosted glass basin hanging from the ceiling flooded the dining room with bright, yellow-white light.

It must have been wintertime because there was to be ice cream—homemade ice cream that Uncle Roland had made that day—and we only had homemade ice cream when the pond was frozen over.

It was always a family endeavor. My brother, Win, would cut the ice and haul it up to the house. My job was to run out to the barn and scoop up a bowlful of rock salt crystals we kept on hand for the horses. Grandma mixed the "receipt." Uncle Roland did the cranking and, with watering mouths, the family would look forward to the evening and great heaping dishes of deliciousness. (Yes, that was before electricity.)

I don't remember eating any ice cream that night, but I remember looking forward to it and having a wonderful time, never suspecting that this very celebration was the opening wedge that would finally nudge out all the things I treasured.

I didn't think much about the electricity for long after that first night. We soon got used to the lights and accepted them without thought. Then one day around the first of June, it dealt me its first blow.

It had been a sticky, hot day, and all the way home from school I'd had two lovely pictures in mind. First, I'd have a long drink, a long, cool drink right from the lip of the pump spout, aching cold, spilling and splashing over my face and chin. (I hated the tepid pipe water at school.) Then, I'd pick a box of strawberries and go up on the henhouse roof to eat them. Oh, life was wonderful!

But, as I stepped off the school bus at the end of the lane, I was greeted with a strange *Putt-putt-putt-putt.* I knew it couldn't be the sprayer; that made more of a chugging sound. So I hurried up the lane, around the house and found Grandma and two strange men standing by the the cellar window, out of which projected an L-shaped pipe, coughing and wheezing and putting and puffing, filling the air with awful noises.

I tried to ask what it was, but Grandma and the men were shouting an earnest conversation above the noise and didn't notice me. Besides, it was hot; and I was thirsty.

I went into the back shed, and stopped dead in my tracks. The pump box was gone—the homely, friendly old pump box, big enough for a fellow to sit in, low enough for him to put his feet in one at a time and wash away the dust with breathtaking iciness. There instead, through the open kitchen door, stood a dazzling new sink with a drainboard and brass spigots. High and haughty it

stood, touching only the kitchen floor with the tip of its curly drainpipe.

For a long moment I stood there, staring, numb. Then I took a glass and limply turned the spigot marked "Cold." It spat; it coughed; it hissed; and finally a thin stream of cloudy, tepid, "pipey" water trickled into the glass. I poured it out, watched it snake down the drain, then went out to the henhouse roof, thirst and strawberries forgotten. I felt like I did the time old Laddie died. A part of me seemed gone, somehow. Never again would wide gushes of coolness rush over my wrists, or the back of my neck or on my bare, dusty feet.

Gollies, I thought, *how can anybody get a foot up that high?* ✤

WHERE... SHOULD A FARMER DRAW THE LINE?

You know there are few farmers — and few city people, too — who can have everything they *want.*

Every farmer draws a line.

On one side are the necessities, the things he *must* have to run his farm — food, clothing, seed, gasoline, implements. On the other side of that line are "Luxuries"—things he can get along without, unproductive things, ornamental things. He *wants* them—but he looks upon them as things to be bought some day in the future.

It's a very good system—if that line is drawn at the right place—if the man who draws the line has all the facts in each case, so that he gets the things he *needs* and the things he *wants* on the right side of his line.

On which side is electricity?

At first thought you may say Electricity is a luxury; that you're going to have it some day, but not this year.

But *is* it a luxury?

Three hundred and fifty thousand farmers who use Delco-Light emphatically say: "*No, it is not.*" They say Delco-Light is a *necessity.* They say it's a profit-producer. They say they couldn't get along without

it. They say it has more than paid for itself.

They also say that along with this necessity which saves time and work, and actually increases their farm profits, they got—without any cost—all the luxuries made possible by electricity.

Let us send you the facts now

We want you to get the facts, too. We want to send you our book "The New Way to Farm Profits." You owe it to yourself, your family and your farm to get the facts—*all* the facts—including details of the arrangements by which you can secure Delco-Light on terms that will be satisfactory to you. Send for your copy of this valuable book today. It will convince you that Delco-Light belongs on the "must have" side of the line.

Delco-Light Company also sells and guarantees D-L Electric Water Systems and DELCOGAS for Household and Commercial Use.

PRODUCTS OF GENERAL MOTORS

Delco-Light Company, Subsidiary of General Motors Corp. Dept. K-12, Rochester, N. Y.
You may send me copy of your free book "The New Way to Farm Profits."

Name..
R. F. D...........Town..............................
County..................State.......................

⟩⟩⟩ *Now 350,000 satisfied users* ⟩⟩⟩

DELCO-LIGHT
DEPENDABLE ELECTRIC POWER AND LIGHT

4-H: 1920

By Edna Clow

ould you girls like to win a trip to the International Stock Show in Chicago?" Our father was trying to interest us in 4-H, the young people's part of the new Farm Bureau.

"But that is for boys," we answered. He explained that because there was no 4-H for girls, many were entering boys' 4-H. Father offered to sell us a nice, smooth Hereford calf, just the right age.

Well, why not? He assigned my younger sister, Inez, to the actual feeding and care of the calf, while I was to keep the detailed records and write a summary of the project.

At the time, President Hoover was telling the nation to "Hoover-ize," or gain as much as possible with the least expense; so our calf was named Hoover.

What a pet he became! We fed him special meal, whole milk, grain and hay. His stall was kept clean and he was washed, brushed and curled. We taught him to lead, climbed over him and even hitched him to a little wagon.

My brother had worked two days to make a harness for Hoover. Hoover didn't mind when Clarence slipped it on. Then Clarence slapped him on the rump, the wagon hit his heels, and Hoover took off.

Directly in his path was a small straw stack. Over it he bolted, wagon parts flying in all directions. When he was stopped, the two front wheels were all that remained.

By late summer, we entered him at the Paullina Fair. He took a blue ribbon and was to lead the parade of 4-H beef. He followed us meekly until the band blasted out loud and clear. That was just too much for Hoover. He danced, whirled and balked, and it took both of us to hold him. Finally, a young man came to our aid.

At the auction following the fair, Hoover brought enough money to pay for his feed, pay my father for his purchase, and put $100 each in Inez's and my bank accounts. In the final report, I wrote the calf's story, plus the cost per pound and gain per day, to be turned in at the county Farm Bureau office.

From there, Hoover was sent to Sioux City to be dressed. In a few days, returns arrived by mail. Hoover had dressed out second in Sioux City and we shouted with joy—the trip was indeed ours! We reread the letter until we came to the words "dressed out"—that means butchered! Our cheers changed to tears. Mother explained how man was given dominion over animals by God, and we had raised him for food.

Now to prepare for the trip. The Farm Bureau would pay one ticket only, so our father paid my way, saying Inez was too young to go alone at 11 years old. I was 14 and felt responsible for us both.

The day after Thanksgiving we left by train. A club leader took us to the hotel where 4-H boys and girls had gathered from all over Iowa. We were shy and awed by the soft carpets and electric lights. It was a wonder we slept at all. I cuddled close to my little sister. Already we seemed so far from home.

After breakfast, which we were too excited to enjoy, we boarded our train for Chicago. There were enough 4-Hers and leaders to fill a passenger car on the train. We would be traveling for a day and night.

Our leaders organized mixer games. We sang and talked excitedly about what lay ahead in our week's tour. We felt grown-up when we ordered our dinner from the dining car. This was the life! Soon we forgot that with every click of the rails we were going farther from home.

After supper in the diner, we settled down in our comfortable seats. Excited chatter slowed down and soon sounds slipped by as we slept.

Some of us woke early enough to see the wide Mississippi River. By noon, excitement ran high—we were in the suburbs of Chicago. Even then it took so long to arrive at the depot.

Making sure we left nothing on the train, our leaders instructed each boy to choose a girl

to walk with and help with her luggage. We were divided into groups with a club leader as guide. The girls were soon settled in the New Southern Hotel facing Lake Michigan, and the boys in the YMCA not far away.

There followed five exciting days at the International Stock Show; a tour of the Armour Packing Plant and stockyards; riding in elevated streetcars; spending a day at the fabulous Lincoln Park Zoo; attending a vaudeville show; a banquet honoring 4-Hers; an overnight boat trip on Lake Michigan to Milwaukee, and then traveling back to Chicago on a fast interurban train; riding an elevated streetcar through the slum area where dingy apartments had the back stairs covered with dirty mattresses; then back to our hotels for baths and rest for our trip home.

We were amazed at the dirt and soot of the city. We craned our necks at high buildings and looked for hours at the flashing electric signs as they changed colors to reflect into our hotel rooms at night. The Wrigley building was most spectacular.

One last adventure was to take an elevator to the very top of the Marshall Field store and look over Lake Michigan where boats looked like toys. We were allowed spending money to purchase a gift for those at home.

On Friday evening, city-weary youngsters boarded the train for Iowa. We were only too glad to leave the noise, dirt and mobs of the big city. No more would we be frightened speechless when our group and leader got off the streetcar at the wrong station.

Coming home meant saying good-bye to friends who shared an adventure with us. Handshakes, hugs and promises to write were soon in the background as our train speeded ever nearer to Sutherland. When the conductor called "Sutherland!" never did our little town and waiting parents look so good.

For the next two days, all we did was eat, sleep and talk. It had been a learning experience beyond comparison. ❖

Pig Races on the Farm

By Alfred E. Ross

I often think of the pig races we staged when I was growing up on a farm in the years before the first World War. They were never-to-be-forgotten memories of an era of my life that have never faded, in spite of passing time and all the other memorable events which have been added since.

I would venture to say that very few people, outside of the few boys who lived on neighboring farms and the few children who accompanied their parents on a summer vacation on our farm, ever attended a pig race or had any part in running one.

I would go further and declare the only place where pig races were staged was at the Clinton Farm, which was one of several milk-producing farms surrounding the village of Pleasant Valley, in New York. These races were not intended to amuse strangers or sports looking for a medium to lay bets, but were planned merely for the excitement and pleasure of several boyhood chums, and the occasional two or three children who came to our farm for a brief stay with their parents during the hot weather.

These races were not intended to amuse strangers or sports looking for a medium to lay bets, but were planned merely for the excitement and pleasure of several boyhood chums.

In those days, country people provided most of their own food. Dairy cows were our main source of cash income, but we also had fruits and vegetables, chickens, ducks, geese and a herd of 15 or 16 pigs of mixed breed and color.

In late spring and throughout the summer, the hogs were turned out to range and root in a fenced field through which a never-failing stream meandered quietly.

This stream was a magnet for both the pigs and those of us who lived in its vicinity. For us, it was a retreat where we could swim and horseplay in the invigorating water, and then emerge to lie on our backs on the bank and gaze at the deep blue of the sky, sometimes watching the lazy, circling flight of an eagle in the faraway distance above us.

For the pigs it was a place where, during the heat of the day, they could take to the water and roll and wallow in the mud and plaster themselves from head to foot until they looked like they had been dipped in a pool of molten chocolate. The mud dried quickly, cracking and making them itchy. Then they would hustle as fast as their short legs could carry them to the nearest fencepost or tree trunk and rub furiously up and down, from side to side, until every particle of mud was brushed from their bodies.

In those halcyon days of our youth, we did not give any thought about the reasons for their actions—that what they did was their way of cleaning themselves and disposing of the biting flies. Even so, they also enjoyed their wallowing in the mud and slime and vigorous massaging, for sometimes they repeated the performance during the day and sometimes two or three times when the weather was hot and humid, and the flies more numerous than usual.

After giving themselves their customary massage with satisfied grunts, they proceeded to pick a cool spot somewhere under the shade of a large tree, and once settled, they soon fell sound asleep for a length of time, unless they were disturbed.

It was during one midsummer day that the idea of a pig race came to mind. We had been splashing about in the water and were sitting on the bank, watching the pigs performing, when the thought occurred that we might run them in a race.

It was a couple of hours after noon. The hogs had finished their wallow and massage and were heading toward the trees at the far end of the field for a snooze. Sometime later in the afternoon they would end their sleep and expect to be

fed, for they were always given some grain each day, even though they had been turned out to grub and graze at will. I knew from past experience that they would come running to the feed troughs when I gave them a pig call from the barnyard.

Next each of us had to select the pig we wanted for our runner in the race. I knew we had to wait until they were oblivious of our presence, and also that we had to be careful not to awaken even a single hog, since only one startled pig was all it would take to alarm the others and send them off in a panic.

I cautioned everybody to be quiet. Without making any noise, each person taking part in the race chose his runner. Then we quietly withdrew in a group and proceeded to the finish line, the feed trough, where grain was placed in the usual quantity for them.

When all was ready and everyone was stationed where they could see everything, I gave the starting signal—the pig call, a piercing "PO-O-O-IE!" which started on a high musical note that was sustained as long as possible and then gradually ended in a somewhat lower range.

At the first call, the pigs all sprang to their feet and listened with ears cocked. When they heard the call repeated, they took off with a rush for the barn. The race was on and there was pandemonium.

First, one boy yelled the call with all his might; then another. Then three or four of us gave chorus to the yelling.

"PO-O-O-IE! PO-O-O-IE! PO-O-O-IE!"

"Come Floppy! Come on, come on!"

"Come on Blackie! PO-O-O-IE!"

"Curly, Curly! Run, Curly, run!"

"Come on Whitie! Come on, Whitie! Hurry, hurry, hurry!"

"Pig, pig, pig!"

"Come on Whitie! PO-O-O-IE! PO-O-O-IE! PO-O-O-IE!"

"Come on, Curly!"

"Come on, Floppy!"

"Come on, Blackie!"

"There's Brownie! There's my pig! Brownie, Brownie, Brownie!"

"Pig, pig, pig!"

"Come on, Brownie! Run, Brownie, run!"

Agitated and urged on by all the shouting and calling, the entire herd came grunting and pounding down the pasture as fast as they could run. No racehorse competing for a prize was ever stimulated any more than those hogs rushing toward the barnyard for their feed. They moved like things possessed. Sometimes one took the lead and held it a few moments, and then another, but usually it was a wild scramble, a hustling and puffing and jostling and crowding and change of positions all the way down the pasture.

That was when the excitement reached a pitch, when there was the most shouting and laughing, for no one could be sure which pig would forge ahead and hold the lead, or fall behind, or make a final plunge and reach the trough first and dive with a squeal for the feed.

Of course, when that happened, the winner was promptly declared and the whole performance was over for that day. There was never any chance of a second race until the pigs took to their basin in the stream and treated themselves to a mud bath and massage, and a snooze in their usual resting place. That would not happen until another day.

It was great fun and a sport which had been self-devised at no cost to anyone. It was also a worthwhile pastime, since it provided a diversion from the routine of farm life.

Beyond the interest and excitement generated by the sport, there is something else that might be mentioned about the race, and that is the psychological benefits accrued. Our parents encouraged us early in life to do for ourselves what children now expect and, in fact, demand others do for them. We were taught to

Wheeling Fence

Full Gauge Wires of

COP-R-LOY
Reg. U. S. Pat. Off.

THE COPPER ALLOYED STEEL

Armored with PURE ZINC

Perhaps you have not given much thought to fencing, but your hard-earned money goes into it for the express purpose of increasing the dividends from the place. Why not put up fencing that will be as permanent at reasonable cost as modern metallurgical science can devise?

Wheeling Fence is this kind. Strong, flexible with the famous Hinge-Joint, it has the feature of increased durability due to the copper alloyed steel, COP-R-LOY, of which it is made. This rust-resisting metal is further protected by a thoroughly applied zinc coating. All Wheeling Fence is tested daily at the factory by being erected just as you put it up on the farm. It comes to you ready to eliminate fence troubles and expense.

Ask your dealer about this fence carrying the registered Wheeling trademark, the identity of many other items made of COP-R-LOY for long life on the farm.

WHEELING CORRUGATING COMPANY · *Wheeling, West Virginia*
Branches: New York   Buffalo   Philadelphia   Chicago   Kansas City   St. Louis
Richmond   Chattanooga   Minneapolis   Des Moines   Detroit   Columbus, Ohio

Save with Steel

Ⓦ **Wheeling**
CORRUGATING COMPANY

CHANNELDRAIN ROOFING
For a lifetime of trouble-free roofing service apply Channeldrain. Made of COP-R-LOY, a rust-resisting steel with two to several times greater life than plain steel. Channeldrain Roofing is built to outlast the building on which it is placed end to give you full protection against fire, lightning and leaks. Easily applied with hammer and nails. See your Wheeling dealer.

be resourceful and independent. Consequently, what we did for amusement individually and collectively was nothing more than the training we received at home and a reflection of the character and wisdom of our fathers, who endowed us with the freedom of thought and action we enjoyed in the small, isolated communities and open spaces on the farms. ❖

Father's Day

By Norman M. Cheney

It was a beautiful July morning. We had finished the chores. It was Sunday morning and we hoped to have the rest of the day off.

Father ruined that hope when he announced at the breakfast table that we were facing an emergency. He explained, "The corn crop is planted, but we have had no rain for six weeks. We have to work on the irrigation canal we have planned."

Our hopes for a swim were dashed. Yet, Father very seldom asked us to work on Sunday.

When we finished eating, we loaded the wagon with tools and drove to the pasture. We parked the wagon in the shade near the dam. Unhitching the horse, we turned him loose to browse.

Dad showed us where and how deep he wanted us to dig the canal. We set to work as the day became hotter.

The cows gathered. Curious about our actions, they formed a ring around us and watched with solemn faces, chewing their cuds rhythmically. Bill and I laughed and shooed them out of the way.

Meanwhile, Dad was digging frantically at a huge white rock. Bending over to lift it out, he offered a magnificent target for Bridget, our 8-month-old heifer. When she saw the perfect target, she lowered her head and butted Father sprawling on his face.

No one was hurt except Father's pride. We laughed politely, but later when we were alone, we roared at the look on Father's face when he picked himself up.

We resumed digging in the terrific heat. We were both soaking with sweat. Father straightened up painfully and glanced at his Ingersol. He said firmly, "My Godfrey! It's 4 o'clock! Boys, how about a swim before supper?"

Surprised, I answered, "I didn't know you could swim, Dad! You never have been swimming with us."

He smiled and replied, "There are many things you don't know about your father. Let's get going."

We drove home rapidly and scooted upstairs for our swimming trunks.

It didn't take long to reach the pond, with Father urging Dick on every time he slowed. Hitching the horse to a tree, Bill and I ran into the brush to put on our tights.

I had just finished when I heard the splash. Bill's head was up; he heard it, also.

We both ran out, as Father dived in and started swimming across the narrows. What amazed us the most was his swimsuit. He was wearing his long winter underwear. Standing in shallow water, he waved and swam back.

I said to Bill, "Now I've seen everything." Bill grinned and nodded his head. ❖

It's Nice to Remember

By Helen E. Waters

Remember the dusty, narrow lane that ran uphill from the main road and led to Uncle Joe's farm? And where it dipped down to the creek beside the ancient cottonwoods and crossed the rattly bridge? And remember the squawking hens as they scattered in alarm in front of the car?

And remember the farm bell that hung in the crotch of the oak tree behind the house and how once in a while you were permitted to pull the rope that sent its deep voice rolling and echoing across the hills?

Remember the little bedroom at the top of the steep stairs, and the dormer windows? And the wonderful view of the tangled garden from the window—the rosebushes and the hollyhocks nodding their heads in the fence corners? When you were downstairs or outside, you could hardly find them for the weeds, but from upstairs they were beautiful.

And remember when Aunt Frances fried doughnuts on the old wood stove and fished out "holes" for you to roll in sugar and pop into your mouth, all hot and savory? And the fun you had pumping water for her at the kitchen sink?

And remember how you'd watch Uncle Joe milk the Jersey cow out in the dark coolness of the barn, and then you'd follow him down into the cellar where he'd pour the milk into the separator? But before it went into the separator, remember the tin cup full of frothy milk he'd give you? And the time he forgot your cupful and later filled it from the two spouts of the separator—some milk and some cream—but you wanted milk "out of a cow, not out of a machine"?

Remember how the barn cats congregated by the cistern for their chance at the still-warm skim milk before Uncle Joe took it to the squealing piglets? And remember the pop that Aunt Frances raised by a pulley out of the cold depths of that cistern on a hot summer's day?

Remember wandering the length of the old neglected summer kitchen and the tool sheds and machine shop connected to it, poking curiously at the old crocks and rusty tools discarded in some bygone era, shying from spiders and webs, until at last you came out the door at the end of the building to find the grindstone, there to climb on its rusty metal saddle and pedal to your heart's content?

Remember how you'd walk lazily up to the big pasture gate and climb to the top rail and gaze across the gently rolling hills, dotted with grazing horses and cattle, and pretend it was yours, all yours?

Then, remember how you'd walk up to the big pasture gate and climb to the top rail and gaze across the gently rolling hills, dotted with grazing horses and cattle, and pretend it was yours, all yours?

And how you'd walk up the slope to the orchard, while the grown-ups sat around wasting their time inside. And you'd find a low crotch in an old tree and sit there looking across the sweltering cornfields and dream dreams of how it would feel to own all this beauty. You'd chew carefully on the sour, wormy apples you'd found on the ground beneath the tree.

And remember the day you were brave enough to crawl under the fence and wander to the far end of the farm where you discovered another little creek, and you sat all alone for some moments watching minnows flitting back and forth between pools, and listening to the tinkle of a miniature waterfall? And how, upon returning, you left the safety of the open, mowed stubble field to walk a little way into the cornfield, with the tall corn swaying above your head, rustling in the breeze?

Will you ever forget the day they took the calf away from the old red cow? You hid in the corncrib, peeping out between the slats while she ran around the farmyard, bellowing and kicking her heels up, threatening anything or anyone she saw. And remember how you were afraid to venture out, but scared to stay inside because you thought you heard rats and mice rustling in the drying ears of corn?

And remember running from the big white rooster who ruled the yard? And finding eggs in the hollow tree? And hunting new kittens in the haymow above the barn, in the fragrant hay, while old Daisy and Ted and Mac and Snip, the draft horses, munched their grain, snorting softly?

Remember how Uncle Joe let you "drive" the team as it hauled hay to the barn, and how you were once permitted to guide them when they were hitched to the contraption on the neighboring farm that ground corn as they walked 'round and 'round in a circle? Of course, in both cases, no one needed to "drive" them, but you pretended you did.

Remember the night when you were older and felt brave and slept till midnight in the hay barn, then gave up and walked across the moonlit yard to the house because the heat of the hay and the rustling of mice kept you awake?

Remember back when you were really little and you'd snuggle closer to your mother or dad as you sat on the farmhouse porch at night, watching hundreds of fireflies and listening to the shivery voices of the screech owls in the woods? And remember how you loved, too, the chorus of frog voices down along the creek?

And then, remember how you hated to be bundled, tired and sleepy, into the family car to make the long trip back to town, along the River Road, and away from the farm you loved so dearly?

It's nice to remember. ✤

Barn Raising, 1910

By J.J. Gotch

One of the most exciting times on a farm, years ago, was "Barn Raising." Barns were built quite frequently in the good old days, simply because so many of them burned up, either by being struck by lightning or fires caused by kerosene lanterns falling over and starting the blaze. After electricity was installed, the fires were less frequent.

Next to threshing time, I reckon the barn raising was pretty exciting. It was a red-letter day on the kitchen calendar.

This engineering feat called for much planning as the basement had to be built first, usually with field stones right off the farm. Then the huge beams and crosspieces, the rafters, etc., all had to be made, drilled to fit the matching beams and pieces. Strong oak pins had to be made to hold the beams and sections together. Later on, some folks used steel bolts that made it much easier.

Generally speaking, the frame of the big barn was all cut and fitted together right on the ground and then the beams were taken apart at the corners, leaving four walls of beams to be raised into position and fitted together into a four-sided frame. The frames for each side were raised with brute strength, a little at a time. Then long poles, with spikes on the top ends, were used to push the big beams into a vertical position. Ropes held by men kept the frame from tipping too far.

After the parts were all tied together with the oak pins or the long bolts, the rafters were hoisted up and place into position. Usually the most experienced men were considered to be the leaders or barn-raising bosses. A good, level-headed leader with 25 to 30 men could erect the frame and have most of the roof on a barn between sunrise and sunset, provided there was no rain or any accidents.

The barn shown in the picture was one of many erected in the Mecosta area near Rodney, Mich. A farmer felt himself slighted if he were not invited to help at a barn raising years ago.

The farm women also had an important part of the job. They provided the food for the midday dinner and the lunch in the afternoon, besides the supper after it was all over in the late afternoon. Fried chicken, homemade bread, cookies, pies, fried potatoes and garden-grown vegetables were, for the most part, standard foods on the farm tables.

All took great pride in their part of the work. The great wooden beams rose up into place, inch by inch, to form the most important building on a farm.

Getting the roof boards on the barn was perhaps the most joyous part of the task. The frames and the roof were the most important things of the day; and, as a climax, there was the great farm dinner at the end of the job—chicken and homemade bread, dumplings and vegetable soup. Those were the days! ❖

Summers on a Country Farm

By Ruby L. Owens

Some of the best parts of my life were spent in the home of my great-grandparents during summer vacation. I know the values of the way of life, the ways of love in the home, I learned from being with the older generation. I do admit, I was a little spoiled, being the only youngster with all adults; but I loved it.

At Grandma's house, the day began early, building a fire in the cooking stove and making a cup of coffee. Coffee tasted so good, as the coffee beans were bought green, then roasted in a heavy iron skillet until just right, then ground in a coffee mill so you always had a good, fresh cup of coffee. Grandma let me have a cup of coffee in the morning, but added sugar and lots and lots of milk to it, so we called it coffee milk.

Fresh eggs, sausage or bacon, grits and hot biscuits were on the menu for breakfast, with plenty of fresh-churned butter, jelly and preserves. There was honey, too, as Grandpa would find a bee tree in the woods and rob it of its honey. Grandpa had a syrup mill so we had sorghum or sugar cane syrup. I felt sorry for the mule; being blindfolded, he would walk around, turning the machinery to press the juice out of the stalks. This juice was cooked in a large vat until thick. It was delicious.

After breakfast was over and the kitchen was in good order, it was time to go to the garden to gather fresh vegetables for dinner. Extra vegetables were canned to be used during the winter months. The pantry shelves were always full of canned vegetables, jams, jellies and preserves. Pickles and chow-chow were made, too. This used all the extra cucumbers.

Ham, bacon and sausages were smoked in the smokehouse. Hog butchering was a busy time for everyone. Lard or shortening was rendered when hogs were butchered. Part of the meat was ground and put through a sausage mill to make links to be smoked; part of the ground meat was molded into small patties and fried, then layered with hot lard into large crocks. This preserved the meat for a period of time.

I know the values of the way of life, the ways of love in the home, I learned from being with the older generation.

After dinnertime was over, it was rest time for everyone. The menfolks, as a rule, stretched out on the porch for a nap. The bedrooms were hot as most of them had only two small windows. At 3 o'clock it was coffee time; then the menfolks went back to the fields.

Suppertime was just to finish up the leftovers from dinner. There were always biscuits and corn bread, and a bowl of corn bread and sweet milk was very good. There was always plenty of fresh milk, and I remember Grandma letting a big crock of milk turn to clabber. The cream was skimmed off the top to churn into butter, and the sour milk, or clabber, put into a cheesecloth bag and hung up to drip. It made the best kind of cottage cheese.

Chicken was on the menu for Sunday. The chickens were put in a coop for several days before they were killed and dressed. At Grandma's I can remember the chicken door had to be closed at night after the chickens all went to roost, or varmints out of the woods would get in and kill them.

One summer an old hen hid her nest under the house and brought out only one chick. It was given to me to care for. I kept the chick in a shoebox on the windowsill by my bed at night, and in a small coop in the daytime. I spent lots of time with the chick until it became a real pet. I named my chick Lucky Lindy, and it did turn out to be a rooster. This was about the time Charles Lindbergh flew his plane, the Spirit of St. Louis, from New York to Paris. When Lindy was old enough, I would talk to him and ask him to crow. He would stretch his neck and crow.

When I went home I had to keep him in a separate yard, as he and Mother's rooster would fight. He lived a long life for a chicken, and when he died we all cried and we gave him a special funeral—even put flowers on his grave.

Monday, weather permitting, was wash day. A fire was started under a big black wash pot which was filled with water. The white clothes were always boiled. This was a long, hard day, as water had to be hand-pumped and carried to the tubs. Besides water in the boil pot, a washtub and two rinse tubs had to be filled. Homemade lye soap was used and the old

washboard really got a good workout.

Flatirons or black irons heated on the cookstove were used to iron the clothes that had to be pressed. In later years when Grandma bought a coal-oil stove, the chore of ironing was much improved, as this was a much cooler way of heating the irons. When I could talk Aunt Emma into letting me press Uncle Van's handkerchiefs, he would brag on me, and when he rode horseback about once a week to the general store and post office, he would bring me a bag of candy, mostly peppermint sticks.

In the wintertime, fireplaces were used for heating, burning up your front and freezing your backside.

I loved life in the country. There was time to enjoy visits from neighbors, and Sundays were the day for family gatherings. Women had time to do a lot of handwork, such as sewing and quilting. Crochet edgings were added to pillowcases and dresser scarves and even slips and panties. After supper was cleared away, we all sat on the porch and talked. A fire was started in an old tub with rags to make good smoke, to keep the mosquitoes away.

Everyone retired early on the farm. Come daylight, everyone but me was up and ready for a new day. ✤

Dry-Land Wheat Farming

By Frank W. Elmore

I'll start this in the summer, the year around 1919. Place is in eastern Oregon on a wheat farm. School was out and I was a lone child on about 360 acres of wheat land. The only other youngster around was a girl two miles away where we went for our cistern water. I would go for the ride and thrill of watching a huge one-cylinder engine with flywheels higher than my head pump water with a *Bang, sputt, sputt, bang, sputt* sound as it filled the tank on our wagon. This water was never wasted. Bath or dishwater might be used to scrub a porch or water a small garden, but it never was just thrown out.

Often I would be given a hoe and sent out to cut tumbleweeds in the fields of new wheat. Through the summer these weeds would fill the gullies and draws as they dried and the winds tumbled them. These same winds would pick up talcum-like dust till you could hardly see. Often after Mother cleaned house, a whirlwind, as we called it, would come spinning across a field and destroy all her work.

Harvest time was the high point of my summer—the extra help to talk with, the chance to ride the combine.

They alternated fields each year. While some were growing, others were being plowed. The plows circled the fields working toward the center, herding jacks (jackrabbits). This was great fun for me as I chased them, and the smaller the area the more rabbits and fun.

Harvest time was the high point of my summer—the extra help to talk with, the chance to ride the combine (Harvester). To me, this was an enormous machine. It was pulled by six or eight teams. The driver sat out over the first team on a wooden framework. Another man kept the combine leveled as they went along hillsides. Believe me, in those days the farmer used every bit of ground. The "sack sewer" was king of the roost. He drew top pay as his speed decided how fast the outfit moved. He filled, jigged (shook down), sewed and placed the sacks in a chute. When full, he'd dump them to be picked up in wagons and hauled to town. I liked to ride with them and trip the chute or pull the rope to dump the chaff at his signal.

Often the drivers let "the kid" ride to town on a load of wheat. Town was a general store, including post office, schoolhouse, granary and depot made of an old boxcar mounted on railway ties, as this was a branch line.

We usually went to bed with the chickens and listened to the howl of the coyote, as we had no radio, phonograph or musical instruments and little to read. Some nights we stayed up late and watched the heat lightning as it lit up the sky or silhouetted the surrounding hills.

Fall meant school and renewed friendships. Most of us rode a horse and our first chore was the care of our horse in the shed provided before we went to class.

Our classroom was a one-room school with one teacher for all eight grades. While one grade recited, the others did assigned work. There wasn't any fancy grading based on the smartest kid, like nowadays. The teacher gave us 10 problems or questions. If we got them all correct, our grade was 100. This went for arithmetic, spelling, history or whatever we were studying.

With the approach of winter, the teacher selected a cast for a play to be presented about Christmastime. This was a big event for the community. The men fixed up a stage in the closest grain warehouse, placed sacks of wheat around the wall for seats, and piled the balance in the far end.

On the big night, families came from near and far in all types of transportation, wagons, buggies and a Model-T or two. The women took foods to the house and exchanged gossip while the menfolk took care of the teams and we kids got in the way.

Once the evening was under way, the school play, with many forgotten lines and coaching from the wings, was presented. This over, the musicians took over the stage and dancing started. If the teacher happened to be a schoolmarm that year, there was a lot of cutting in by the young bucks. Around midnight the food was served. Dancing was soon under way again with a mother taking time out to bed a sleepy youngster down on the sacks at the far end of the building. No one went home till dawn on this night. They couldn't if they wanted, as there were no headlights on a wagon.

The winters in eastern Oregon could be rough, snowdrifts so high we could hollow out a cave high enough to stand in. Thawing and freezing formed a crust hard enough to support a horse if it stepped gingerly. I had a homemade sled of heavy wood with runners of buggy wheel steel. I'd pull this to the top of a hill, and once on the way down there was no steering or stopping on the ice crust.

Spring brought mud hub-deep to a wagon wheel, with many roads washed out. Evenings were spent doing homework, playing rummy, solitaire or some card game by the light of a coal-oil lamp. If we had to go, the "little house" after dark was a thrill for a kid. Our imaginations ran wild as we sat there by candlelight. When we headed for the house, we made tracks—we just *knew* something was following us.

Things gradually dried out. The chickens hid their eggs in weed nests which we had to find before the crows did. Summer moved in, tumbleweeds, rattlesnakes, jackrabbits and other wild things came to life, and we were on our way again. ✤

Father and the Flying Machine

By Harold W. Wait

One sweltering July afternoon in 1923 we were loading hay in the east meadow just beyond the cornfield.

Father was on top of the load. He always seemed to be at a point from which he could direct the actions of the rest of us.

Waldo, the hired man, was pitching on. Father loaded 'round and 'round, big tumbles for the corners and double binding in the middle. Father made a load of hay the way they built the vault in the First National Bank—square and sturdy—and without the right combination you could hardly unload it.

As usual, I, at age 9, was the low man of the crew. My job was raking scatterings. This was the first task allotted a boy just barely big enough to help with haying. I was dragging that miserable contraption known as a bull rake—5 feet wide with teeth a foot long.

"Keep close to the cart and rake clean." Those were Father's instructions and he made sure they were carried out.

When I arrived at the cart with a rakeful of scatterings, no one wanted to bother with them. Waldo didn't like to pitch them on, as they wouldn't hold together well and got chaff down his neck. Father didn't like them because they couldn't go anywhere except in the middle and that interrupted his loading plan. I could not understand, since they both disliked scatterings so much, why we bothered with them; but bother we did. I was continually urged to hurry up with those scatterings, but when I got there, I would be told, "Don't dump them here. Go around to the other side of the load."

Even old Laddie, the shepherd dog, relaxing in the shade under the wagon, had a look on his face that said he preferred his role to mine.

We were half-loaded and I wondered if we would ever make it back to where the Bennington jug of ginger drink was hidden in the shade, when I heard a loud buzzing in the sky. It increased in volume, and I finally located the source. It was Captain Stickney's airplane.

Captain Stickney, who had been a pilot in the war, used to land in any open field and take up passengers. He was heading directly for our cornfield. The corn was a foot high and probably, from the air, appeared to be a smooth green carpet.

As the plane came nearer and the buzzing became louder, Chub and Molly, the horses, began to show alarm. The flies had been bothering them and here was the king of all flies, diving right at them. They snorted and reared and, in trying to get away from this gigantic insect, tipped the hayrack, depositing Father on the ground with the load of hay on top of him. Father burst out of the hay fighting mad and, shouting to Waldo to hold the horses, he brandished his pitchfork and charged into battle.

Captain Stickney had been able to cope with the enemy during the war, but he was not prepared for an embattled farmer with a pitchfork. He zoomed into the sky, banked around and headed for friendlier territory, landing in the next field belonging to our neighbor, Mrs. Allen.

Father came back to the wagon, slapping the dust from his hat which had been blown from his head by the wind from the plane.

Swearing was not allowed on our farm; in fact, one hired man had been fired for breaking this rule. To my surprise, Father not only knew all the cuss words I had ever heard, but several that were new to me, and he delivered them with a force and fluency I had never heard. I decided then and there that it was a good idea to know the words, and that holding them in reserve for a real emergency made them much more effective.

People were gathering around the plane and Father, somewhat mollified by his victory over the captain, told me I could go over and see it.

Near the plane I met Mrs. Allen's grandson Jimmy, and as it was our first close-up

glimpse of a plane, we really looked it over. It was a biplane, made mostly of wood and canvas with a lot of guy wires holding it together. The captain, in his riding boots and breeches, leather jacket and helmet with his goggles pushed up on his forehead, surely was a heroic figure. Two of the biggest boys had the post of honor; they held the wings.

Captain Stickney, after placing the passenger in the cockpit, stepped up to the polished wood propeller. He whirled it once—nothing happened; twice, and the engine coughed; the third time the engine burst into life and the whirling propeller became a blur.

The captain climbed into the plane, pulled down his goggles and waved to the boys to release the wings. Away went the plane, bumping over the meadow and at last becoming airborne. The flight cost $5 for five minutes, and although $5 was two days' pay, the captain was doing a good business.

The captain offered Mrs. Allen a free ride to pay for the use of the field, but she said that, having lived a good life, she expected in a few years to go far higher than Captain Stickney was ever apt to, so she would let her grandson Jimmy have the ride. Mrs. Allen said that as Jimmy was so small, she would not be getting full value and I should go along, too.

Soon we were strapped in and bumping over the meadow. When the bumping stopped and we dared to look over the side, the field was far below. Flying up the valley, we tried to identify the houses that looked so small and different. When we came to the church, we dove down and went around the steeple on a level with the clock.

Heading back for a landing, we passed over our farm. Far below me were Father and Waldo, going back to the field. That was the biggest thrill of the whole flight. ✛

Grandma's Summer Kitchen

By Joyce C. Rose

G randma's summer kitchen was located in the back addition of her large, white, weathered farmhouse. The Quackenbush homestead, nestled in a forest of pine trees, was shaded well, with the summer kitchen protruding into this coniferous display—a cool retreat on a hot summer day. The furnishings in Grandma's summer kitchen were for practicality only. This room was the "work kitchen," and as such, not required to adhere to the normal rules of the house. This was a place of convenience and comfort. The grandchildren were especially attracted to it, because we could share in the "summer work" of berry picking, hulling and preserving; vegetable garden harvesting; canning; and freezing. Our little spills and errors were somehow overlooked.

The two-burner gas stove to the right of the door got a thorough workout during the summer. Whether it was fried bread (a granddaughter delicacy), or bubbling raspberry jam, there was usually a delicious aroma. On the other side of the table holding the propane stove was the doorway to the walk-through pantry. Since the door was usually open, the area behind it became a great storage spot for books and magazines. Hence, my paperback world of fantasy to which I often escaped was always available. The rocking chair by that stack of magazines soon became my favorite spot.

Right beside that rocking chair was a window that was usually open. The breeze which flowed between the screen door and that window was so calm, yet so exhilarating. I remember Grandma often pulling her chair over next to mine, wiping the perspiration from her brow. The breeze would flow through at just the right moment.

Often, Grandma would take me on her lap in that old rocking chair. I would lean against her shoulder and feel such peace and love. She would soothe me during my

The kitchen table was on the wall between that stove and the outside door. Here was where we sat to do most of the hulling and picking over of Grandma's berries.

What!

A WAY TO GET 2/3 MORE JELLY?

Yes! Just look what Sure-Jell does!

1 **ONLY ½ MINUTE BOIL** *for jellies;* one minute for jams. You can actually finish a whole batch of jam or jelly in less than 15 minutes after your fruit is prepared! That's one reason women everywhere are so delighted with this new Sure-Jell.

2 **TWO-THIRDS MORE JELLY** *or jam* . . . Because of that extremely short boil, none of the juice boils away. So you actually get two-thirds more jam or jelly . . . as much as 11 *glasses* from the same amount of fruit that gave you only 7 *glasses* the old, "long-boil" way. What a saving in money!

3 **PERFECT RESULTS** *with any fruit; finer flavor, too* . . . No more worry about failures. Sure-Jell eliminates uncertainty. With this wonderful new pectin product, *all fruits* jell perfectly. The flavor is much finer, too. Short boiling retains all the *real* flavor of the ripe fruit. There is no "boiled-down" taste!

MONEY BACK OFFER. Buy two packages of Sure-Jell. Use one. If it does not do all we claim for it, just take the other package back to your grocer. He will refund the full price of both packages. (Sure-Jell is a product of General Foods. You can buy it at any grocer's.)

SURE-JELL 13¢ 2 PACKAGES FOR 25¢

annual bouts with poison ivy, read to me or just talk. Once she said to me, "Honey, will you always sit on Grandma's lap—even when you are big and I am old?"

My response was quick and sure. "Yes, always, Grandma, always."

Next to the rocking chair was a big kitchen wood stove. Grandma rarely used it, as propane was much more convenient and did not heat up the kitchen. The kitchen table was on the wall between that stove and the outside door. Here was where we sat to do most of the hulling and picking over of Grandma's berries. This was the "work kitchen." Oh, it would be cleaned up later. Right then, there was jam to make.

Breakfast was a special time in Grandma's summer kitchen. Grandma would brown her butter in the fry pan before adding the eggs to scramble. Eggs were never so delectable! Add those to freshly toasted bread spread with butter and newly made raspberry jam. Yum!

Grandma's summer table was the source of many simple but memorable meals and snacks. In the middle of the afternoon, my farmer grandfather would come in from his chores, sit down at the back of the table by the stove and treat himself to the delicacy of bread cubes soaked in milk. Many times, I would join him.

Grandma's chair was at the front of the table where she could look out the door and up the path that wound around the corner of the house and toward the barn. One day, around that corner came my tall uncle carrying my moaning, pale grandfather on his back. "Ma, help!" he yelled. "The hay wagon rolled over Pa's foot." My uncle was almost as pale as Grandpa. I was scared! I knew my old-fashioned grandfather did not like doctors. But Grandma quickly got the needed help. Grandpa was out of commission for a while but, with time and the Lord's healing, he got back on his feet.

This path brought friends and family to Grandma's summer kitchen. Because it wound around the corner to the mostly hidden-from-view driveway, it was a big surprise to look out and see visitors. The kitchen was often bustling with activity, but company was greeted warmly.

Grandma's summer kitchen is a source of special memories for me. When I look out the door and up the path, I see a son carrying his injured father on his back. When I look at that old propane stove, I see Grandma stirring bubbling raspberry jam. Behind the pantry door, I see stacks of fantasy. The kitchen table brings back floods of memories of good food and frivolous, but caring, fellowship. And when I look at that old rocking chair, I see Grandma holding a little girl on her lap, and I hear the words, "Always, Grandma, always."

I see love. ✣

Exposing Our Calves

By Mary Lee Reisch Moles

M-A-T-T-I-E!" (That's Blue Ridge Mountain talk for one with the euphonious cognomen of "Martha.") It was our 6-foot, 7-inch Virginian grandfather, with cupped hands, calling to my mother. This method preceded all intercoms, I am certain, and was always effective. "These kids are going to get killed!" he hollered.

My brother Joe, five years my senior, and I, a grown-up 4-year-old, crouched near a manger in one of several huge red barns on Granddad's American Hereford Farm. We silently prayed that our heavy breathing would not reveal just how we were to meet our instant demise.

Mother hurried to the barn, drying her hands on her apron. From our wee peephole, we watched her expression change to one of concern.

Then we heard Granddad reveal our little secret to Mother. Joe and I had earned money by various duties around the farm. We salvaged overripe apples from the ground, peeling them and performing fast surgery on the wormholes before watering them down to make vinegar. This we merchandised at 10 cents per gallon. We were also pretty adept at debugging potato plants, receiving 5 cents a can for the bright orange potato bugs.

They paid off punctually, but rather than accept our earnings in a few 2½ x 6-inch legal tenders of George Washington, we made a deal to apply our earnings on runt calves. We knew they would be abundantly fed, as they shared feed troughs with the others born on the farm, and would become of greater value when the market opened.

This particular day we owned four such calves, and they were housed with just short of 100 other beautiful, innocent-looking, curly, white-faced Herefords, all gamboling together in the huge barn. Joe would hold one of our calves near the wall, pick me up (a pudgy 4-year-old), set me on the calf's back, step aside, and everybody for themselves. I rode this calf until it felt the urge to unload me, but it didn't bother much to fall because I merely landed on other fat, cushiony, bawling calves, picked myself up and was ready for the next ride.

Granddaddy went about his supervision duties, checking other barns, ponds, windmills and separate obstetric quarters. When all was quiet, we again resorted to gaining information at the peephole and saw Mother returning home through her garden gate.

My city-bred engineering father had so recently been transplanted to the farm, and he was most receptive at suppertime when Mother smilingly said, "Daddy, at least we have one equestrian in the family."

My brother and I nearly choked on the country ham, biscuits and gravy as we wondered which one was the equestrian and just what the penalty would be. Did it mean we would have to submit graciously to the ever-present onion cough syrup (always brewing on the back of the Round Oak Range)? Would we get a second washtub bath before Saturday night, or have to practice an additional hour on the tiresome pump organ?

This, too, did pass! Surely we would not go back to "breaking bovines," especially when Granddaddy, with all good intentions, had exposed us and our calves. ❖

Music to Live By

By Audrey Kilchenman

During the hot, sweltering summer days of the Depression years, my father walked behind a team of draft horses as he plowed the rocky Stony Patch. We all toiled with him, planting, hoeing, shocking corn or making hay. As a matter of fact, we did all the things we thought a boy should do; only we had no brothers, so in our family the work was shared by us girls. Perhaps that is why I always remember the music—the music my father taught us to live by—that made the intolerable tolerable.

He taught us to listen to the peepers along the creek in early spring, to the whippoorwill singing in the pear tree at dusk, and to the call of the wild geese honking their good-bye as they headed south in autumn. We heard the song of the bees in the rose bushes and the welcome rhythm of the raindrops on the hot tin barn roof at the end of a scorching day. So day by day, with his help, we found the world alive with music and learned that each of God's creatures plays a part in life's symphony.

He taught us, too, the joy of sharing music with others, and often, when the day's work was ended, neighbors would gather beneath the stars to sing some old songs or learn a new one.

But the best of all memories was when we lived around the piano on holidays. Those special days always found Dad seated beside the pianist, surrounded by his children and, eventually, many grandchildren. He turned the pages and we all sang hymns, carols, some country tunes, then back to hymns again. When we finished singing one of his favorite numbers, he invariably said the same thing: "Let's all sing it again, one more chorus." Everyone laughed and sang with special fervor, and for a little while our world was filled with peace and plenty.

Yes, my Christian father gave us the priceless gift of music to cherish forever. Now when we walk in the fields and forests with our own children, we remember and try to pass the gift along. Once in awhile, as we rest on a hilltop and watch a golden sunset, we can almost hear angels singing beautiful music. They must be. It wouldn't be heaven for Dad without it. ✤

Stacking Hay

By L.A. Stevens

The cool of the morning was gone with the rising sun. Even before breakfast it felt good to be barefoot, to feel the clover still damp and cool underfoot as we went for the cows.

The tall cottonwoods in the grove stood serene—leaves glistening in the sunlight. Quiet and regal they stood with scarcely breeze enough to tremble the leaves of the topmost branches that pierced the blue bowl over our heads.

Later, when we rose from the breakfast table, Father said, "Well, boys, we've got a big day's work ahead of us. Lot of hay down. Get a move on now and we can get right at it." Then he added, "It'll be a scorcher today."

Roscoe and I ran to follow orders. The hired man had harnessed the two black mares we were to hitch to the buggy, and they were waiting for us at the water tank. My brother hitched them up while I filled the jug with cold water from the windmill and wrapped a wet gunnysack around it to help keep it cool.

The pungent odor of drying hay met us halfway to the field in a single breath reminiscent of a summer's work; unpleasant, where it should have been pleasant, because it also made us aware of the task ahead.

We stowed the jug in the shade under the buggy seat. With Roxy, the big Percheron mare we would hitch to the rake, trotting behind us, we started for the field. We were as glad to put on our stiff, clumpy shoes now as we had been to leave them off earlier. They would protect us from the grass stubble and the hot sand.

The sky had faded somewhat. Even by 8 o'clock it seemed to lose its importance against the competition of the sun. The sweat bands of our straw hats were already damp. It would be a scorcher all right. The pungent odor of drying hay met us halfway to the field in a single breath reminiscent of a summer's work; unpleasant, where it should have been pleasant, because it also made us aware of the task ahead.

The stacker had already been placed in front of the old stack bottom, and by the time we arrived, Ed, the hired man, had bunched two or three sweep loads of hay behind it and was out gathering a new load. Sweep rake astraddle a windrow, a horse on each side, the long narrow teeth picking up the hay, Ed gathered a load, brought it in and shoved it onto the stacker teeth.

My job was to drive the stacker team. This team, hitched to a long, stout rope, hoisted the hay onto the stack through a system of pulleys. With the load secure on the double set of stacker teeth, one row at right angles to the other to hold the hay in midair, I slapped the reins. The team began to pull and the load of hay rose in an arc until the stacker stood perpendicular and the hay slid off onto the stack.

Load after load came in, swung up and over and was carefully forked into place. Every few loads Father climbed down the ladder (which still extended far above the stack) to examine the shape of the stack and admire its symmetry.

Back and forth went the sweep. By midmorning, the fly nets on the horses were splotched with sweat. Greenish foam gathered at the sides of the horses' mouths to slobber on the ground when they shook their heads. Perspiration began to spread from under our suspenders, making dark diagonal stripes from waist to shoulder.

By noon the stack stood two-thirds the height of the ladder. Horses turned loose trotted for the barn. We pitched the loose hay away from the stack and tossed it into the rack, ready to be taken home when fully loaded, then climbed in the buggy for the short drive to the house and dinner.

Dinner over, Father hurried us

back to work instead of allowing us the usual rest under the trees. "It's mighty hot to work the horses, but we'd better get going and get that hay up. I don't like the look of things. Beats all, anyway! A hundred and four in the shade. Liable to storm before night. Weather like this could cook up a regular goose-drownder."

The stack was now high enough to cast shade on my side, and also high enough to shield me from Father's disapproving eye. Because the sweep must go farther and farther for hay each trip, I had more time between loads to lie on the stubbly grass, partly smoothed and flattened by now, and read the book I had smuggled to the field in the bib of my overalls.

The stack grew to the top of the ladder and Father made his last trip down for a drink from the brown jug. Resting it on the crook of his elbow, he tilted it and drank. The hired man could do this, too, but try as we might, neither Roscoe nor I could master this trick. When we wanted a drink, we had to put the jug on the floor of the buggy and slowly tip it to the drinking level. The mark of manhood to us was to be able to lift that jug with one hand, let it roll over on the crook of the arm and have a free hand to pull the corncob stopper.

The heat grew more intense. Occasionally a thin white cloud gave momentary relief, sending a sickly shadow scudding across the meadow, gone almost as it came. The birds sought shelter in the uncut grass and trees and almost the only sound came from the clatter of the rake as Roscoe drove old Roxy up and down the windrows, picking up the "scatterings." Every hour or so he would rattle up to the stack for a drink and then follow the sweep out again to gather more leavings. The stack had grown so high it now topped the ladder, and when Father wanted a drink, we tied the jug to the stacker teeth and sent it up with a load of hay.

At about 3 o'clock Mother came out with lunch. This gave us a few moments' respite, too soon over, but dispelling a bit of our weariness.

An hour or so later, I noticed clouds growing above the western horizon. Father must have seen it before I did, but said nothing.

There were still more than a dozen loads to bring in to the stack and no time to waste. The cloud bank rose steadily. Ominous and foreboding, it seemed to blink at us, as much as to say "Hurry up, or I'll soak that hay for you!"

Seven loads still lay neatly windrowed, and the rumblings of distant thunder urged us to make haste. My book forgotten, I cleaned up around the stack and piled the hay ready to be thrown on the rack. I carried the stones to weight down the stack to a convenient spot and brought the ball of twine from the buggy. Then Father called down for me to measure off the twine and tie it to the stones. "There's wind a'coming," he called down. "It'll rip the top clear off if we don't tie 'er down."

Fatigue gave way to the zest of the race. We flung our hats to the ground, leaving damp foreheads to dry in the cooling breeze that came to usher in the storm. Black clouds rolled toward the zenith, rent by crinkly rivers of flame. Apprehensive with each new flash of lightning and roll of thunder, yet thrilled by the uncontrollable terror approaching, we hustled. The last two loads came from the slough. Tough and coarse, this hay was good for naught but to top the stack and shed water from the good hay. Up and over went the last load. Down came the teeth again for the final trip. Ed tied the stones fast and I hoisted them aloft, then Father slung them across the stack

Then came the difficulty. Father must get down to the ground. The top of the ladder leaned against the stack far below him. He must come down on the stacker teeth. I drove the team out the full length of the rope and the hired man held it taut to prevent its slipping. It was a perilous climb to the crotch of the teeth, but even in the face of a storm, it must have been as good as a ride on the Ferris wheel at the county fair. I stood breathless until Father touched the ground, safe, envying him that distinction of being "the man on the stack."

Ed turned the sweep team loose while Father pitched the extra hay onto the hayrack. I hitched the blacks, and when Roscoe clattered in with the rake, I helped him unhook Roxy. Sharper and oftener came the lightning. Each boom of thunder grumbled louder and closer.

I elected to ride Roxy home instead of going with the load of hay. Roxy's 20 years and 1,800 pounds prevented any burst of speed, but the excitement of the approaching storm kept her at a steady clomping trot all the way home.

The team pulling the hayrack trotted in close behind me, and Father shouted to me to close the granary doors and look to the chickens. The sling load of hay on the rack must be pulled through the big barn door into the mow before the storm broke. The wind was rising now. The cottonwoods in the grove thrashed against each other, loosing stray leaves and tiny branches that flew far out over the yard.

The wind turned icy. The saffron sky tumbled eerily. Raindrops left splotches as big as pennies on my shirt as I ran. I reached the shelter of the shed door, then turned and looked back, just in time to see the big barn door closing. The hay was safe. The chores would wait the fury of the storm. ❖

The Empty Bucket

By Roxie Phillips

One beautiful summer morning back in the '30s, I decided to go out looking for wild grapes which then grew pretty plentifully in our Arkansas Ozarks. Usually one or both of our teen-age daughters would have been with me, but later I was glad I had gone alone.

After the farm chores were mostly finished, I donned my sunbonnet and, taking a 3-gallon pail, walked across our 40-acre place, slipping my belt through the bucket bail, freeing my hands for the climb up the steep, timbered mountain ahead.

At the top I came out into the flat field which covered the mountain where, from my earliest memory, had lived a large family. Through death of some and scattering of others, the place was now vacated (of people) and partly overgrown with scrub sprouts.

After walking for some distance toward the vacant house, I noticed to my left a herd of cattle. Hoping they had not sensed my presence, I started pretty pertly in the opposite direction, as sometimes cattle herds are not friendly with strangers, especially with a big brute in the lead.

I had not long to wonder, for by the bellowing and pounding hoofs, I knew they were coming. I ran as fast as my lithe limbs would take me, looking for something for protection.

Some distance ahead I spied a hickory sapling with low limbs for a quick climb up. By the time my feet had reached the height of their backs, they were there, bellowing and pawing up the ground under me. Now you see why I was thankful to be alone. Might a second climber have been too late? Would the little tree have accommodated another's weight?

Through the hours they kept me up there, while they were swaying the sapling and butting the bark from its trunk. I was wondering how much longer it would stand. Finally they gave up and circled out to graze, and then retreated in the direction from which they had come.

I watched them to a safe distance, then I came down and ran from the mountain, coming to and crossing the field of another neighbor and on into the road a mile from our place.

When I reached home that afternoon, the family wondered at my long stay and the empty bucket. I had only a story to tell.

I have since wondered how it would have been had not that hickory sapling stood on that opportune spot, but I'm quite sure I would not now be a great-grandmother writing this. ❖

Apple Cores & Salt Shakers

By Mrs. Edna Clow

*M*other, may we have a salt shaker?" My sister and I would slip one into our pinafore pockets and skip barefoot through the cool grass to the orchard. There, under the Whitney apple tree, we'd shove little hands into crisp, starched pockets to enlarge them enough to be filled with apples. Our Whitneys were best when they were just a little green and crisp enough to snap when we took a bite. The seeds hadn't yet turned brown, and a sprinkle of salt enhanced their sweetness.

With full pockets we perched on the stile that led into the orchard and enjoyed a feast. In spite of the warm summer day, we were cooled by breezes that shifted the mottled shade of spreading apple trees.

In those days, nearly every farm of Highland Community had an apple orchard. Ours was planted by my pioneer grandfather. He was a poor boy from England who had worked his passage and come to northwest Iowa with his covered wagon. He took great pride in his hard-earned farm home and planned it to resemble an English estate. Lawns were landscaped, trees trimmed, and adjoining the farmhouse was a huge orchard and garden surrounded by a high fence. One of my earliest memories was the flowering catalpa trees that faced the road along a half-mile of his farmland. As I look back, it was a beautiful spot to spend my childhood.

Among the apple trees were Greenings. These were large, hard green apples—not good to eat when hand-picked just before frost, but after they were wrapped and packed in barrels to be opened around Christmastime, they were mellow and juicy. Grandmother often set a few on top of the hard coal burner, where they would juggle and dance as they warmed up before we ate them. The room would fill with a sweet, warm, apple aroma.

Another huge apple was the brilliantly red Wolf River. I could never eat a whole one, try as I might. They, too, were too hard and puckering sour to eat before storing. Dad and Grandfather would carry barrels of these to the storm cave. Along toward spring they would bring up icy cold, mellow apples. How good they were, for we couldn't buy the variety of green foods in stores during long winter months. I've never

> *Nearly every farm of Highland Community had an apple orchard. Ours was planted by my pioneer grandfather.*

tasted any like them to this day. We often took them in our school lunch pails. We always lined our lunch baskets up on a bench in the rear of the schoolroom. If a careless student left his lunch in the entry, he found his apple frozen by noon!

Then there were Wealthy apple trees. Their fruit was medium-sized and striped with red when mellow, juicy-ripe. Along midsummer, Dad and Grandfather would clean up the cider press. We helped pick and sort apples—no worm holes please—before they were put through the cider press by the bushel! The foamy fresh cider was delicious. We were right there with our tin cups to catch as much as Mother would let us have.

Fresh cider was stored in huge wooden barrels, or drums, as they were called. They would be lugged to our cool cellar, where a little "mother of vinegar" was added, and in due time, vinegar would be sold—part of the farm income. I faintly recall a hired man who frequently turned the bung, or faucet, on a drum to sample the hardening cider. One hot evening he sampled too much. Dad made him sleep in the barn!

But Wealthies were used for more than cider. They made clear, tangy green applesauce. Mother's spicy green apple pies filled the kitchen with a tantalizing flavor. Topped by a scoop of homemade ice cream or a wedge of yellow cheese—we'd better not go into that! Frozen apple pies or bakery strudels of today cannot hold a candle to them! In early September evenings we'd return from school to the cinnamon aroma of golden apple butter bubbling in a huge kettle on the stove. Next winter, along with Mother's feathery hot biscuits, oh boy! No wonder I was a chub!

Another favorite apple was Iowa Blush. Today it would be called Golden Delicious. We waited impatiently until Grandfather decided

they had ripened enough. Then they were hand-picked, perfect crisp apples, wrapped and stored in the storm cave. Here was another use for the Sears catalog!

I must not forget the crab apple trees. Their fruit was small, hard, brilliantly red and puckery sour! But I recall the shelves of red apple jelly, clear as a jewel and mild to taste. Remember, this was before we could buy pectin to make sure the jelly would set. Yet it did! Roll jelly cake with fresh cream was special.

Among other summer chores was making apple pickles from Whitneys. Each little apple had to be perfect, for it was pickled whole. If cooked just right, the apple skin would remain smooth and plump. After a month or so in spicy pickling syrup, they were delicious, especially with meat.

The land was young, the trees well cared for and fruit was nearly perfect. We were not troubled with worms, moths, blights or disease in the young trees.

Today the orchard is gone, but when we drive by that farm I don't see it as it is, but as it was! We were, indeed, fortunate! ❖

Summertime on the Farm

By Phyllis Sweet Ely

ummertime and the living is easy." So goes the George Gershwin tune in *Porgy and Bess;* but not so for the farmer in New England. I grew up on a farm in the Berkshire Mountains in Massachusetts and it was anything but easy living during the summer months.

On a farm, the busiest time of the year starts in April and continues until the beginning of October when the last of the cornstalks are plowed under. The day begins at 5:30 a.m. and ends anytime after dusk.

Ours was a very active farm. We had the usual dairy cows, but our main source of income was the poultry. They produced thousands of eggs which my father took to market. The eggs had to be taken from the nests of some rather nasty hens, who liked nothing better than pecking at tender fingers. The eggs were taken to the egg room

On the farm, the day begins at 5:30 a.m. and ends anytime after dusk.

where they were washed, candled, weighed and boxed, with the undersized or not-so-perfect eggs put aside to be sold to restaurants. This job was delegated to the female siblings in my family as the boys had to do the more physical, masculine work in the barn and out in the fields. Sometimes we girls wondered who had the better job.

We also had acres of strawberries that needed to be picked and boxed for marketing. This job was too big for the eight of us, so my father hired kids from town to help. Once a good group was hired, we would troop to the fields which, of course, had to be in the direct sun all day.

By the time the sun reached its noon peak, we were not only exhausted from picking and eating strawberries, but our skin was as red as theirs. At this time the town kids would be given an hour to rest and we would help my mother prepare the noonday meal. It was a job I usually disliked as I preferred doing outdoor chores (being the tomboy of the family), but I must admit that after being in the hot field all morning, it was a pleasure to be inside the cool kitchen of our farmhouse. The hour seemed to fly though, and before long it was time to go back into the field again for more berry picking.

There was a smaller berry field down the road from the house and my father would let us pick the berries there for our pocket money. This was a lot of fun. Unlike picking in the main field where we were under the watchful eye of my mother, we were on our own and would sing, throw berries at one another and wait for the bread man to come over the hill.

We would hail him to stop so we could look over his wares and see which delectable morsels we could indulge ourselves in. The jelly doughnuts always won out.

Once the berries were picked, we would sit in front of the house taking turns selling our wares. Word spread quickly about our berries and it took only a couple of hours to sell a morning's worth of strawberries.

Haying season was in full swing by the time the last strawberries were picked. My father was not a man enthralled by modern methods of farming so I remember that, even though most farmers in our area were using a John Deere or Farmall tractor, my father was still using a team of horses by the names of Polly and Molly.

The day came when my father retired the horses to pasture and they were replaced by the "iron horse." All of my older siblings got a thrill from my father allowing them to take a turn driving this new modern convenience, but I think my father and I still yearned for the quiet, steady walk of Polly and Molly.

A short time after the tractor arrived, a new machine called a hay baler came into our lives. This turned rows of freshly mown hay into perfect squares. We were greatly impressed with this cumbersome-looking contraption and haying time was cut in half.

Our farm was sold many years ago and there are no longer the barns and activities I remember, but the memories are so vivid in my mind that when I go to the Berkshires for a visit, one of my first stops is the farmhouse where so many happy memories still live. As unglamorous and hardworking a lifestyle as farming is, there is nowhere else I would have chosen to be brought up as a child. It saddens me to see so few farms in this area now, and I hope there is a way to preserve the ones that are left. ❖

Autumn Days

What was fall on the farm without Thanksgiving Day? Thanksgiving in the Good Old Days was a day of tradition for the Tate family. Christmas was generally reserved for the five of us—Daddy, Mama, Dennis, Donna and I—but Thanksgiving was the day we loaded up and went to Grandpa and Grandma Tate's.

Grandpa and Grandma had 13 children and raised 11 of them to adulthood. Thanksgiving was the holiday when those children and their progeny—usually numbering over a hundred—came to pay honor to Grandpa and Grandma.

Our traditions were very basic and simple. They began with the traditional drive, which often reminded me of Lydia Maria Child's *Thanksgiving Day*: "Over the river and through the wood, to Grandfather's house we'll go; the horse knows the way to carry the sleigh through the white and drifted snow." Of course, the horse and sleigh was our old car.

When I sang the verse, "Over the river and through the wood, now Grandmother's cap I spy. Hurrah for the fun! Is the pudding done? Hurrah for the pumpkin pie!" I *knew* it was talking about our Thanksgiving.

We youngsters were relegated to the out-of-doors. The exception to the "stay outside" rule was the traditional trek of grandchildren and great-grandchildren to the living room of the old house, where Grandpa and Grandma presided over the holiday affair. There was time for a hug and kiss from Grandma and a pat on the head or back from Grandpa—an all-too-quick "I love you!" and we were outside again.

The women and older girls pulled the Thanksgiving dinner together. (Not lunch, *dinner*—supper later would come from the leftovers from dinner.) The men whittled and jawed. A few pitched horseshoes one last time before the quickly approaching winter.

Then it was time. The adults flowed to the front porch, calling to the youngsters who then swarmed like ants to the front yard. Then, on cue it seemed, we bowed our heads as Grandpa asked one of his sons to ask a blessing on the food. As we stood in that front yard of the old farmhouse, heads bowed, I think there was a connection that transcended the four generations that were gathered. Caught in that brief glow of Thanksgiving tradition, we were all one.

After dinner the play was a little more subdued, the talk perhaps a little more philosphical. By the time the day was spent, so were we. The long shadows from the towering oaks in the front yard told us another Thanksgiving Day was over. Another round of hugs for Grandma (Grandpa by this point was too tired for any more pats), a few hasty goodbyes to favorite cousins and we were on our way home again.

Innocently, I thought it would be like this forever. In some ways I guess it has; the faces have just changed. Fall gave us a chance to catch our breath. There was a bit of time between harvest and the harsh realities of winter to reflect on the good parts of the past year. Times were tough, but those crisp autumn days always reminded us we were glad we lived on the farm back in the Good Old Days.

—*Ken Tate, Editor*

My Uncle Was a Thresherman

By Bennie Bengtson

The old steam-engine days of threshing remain with me in many a nostalgic memory all the more vividly because I had an uncle who was a thresherman, and who owned a steam-powered threshing rig.

When a boy, I looked forward eagerly to the fall days when threshing would get under way. As the time neared, my suspense and anticipation burgeoned like the weeds in June. Would the day never come? I slept but little the night before and was out long before dawn to round up the cows for the morning milking. No one needed to call me even once on the morning that Uncle was due to come!

To me, then, the most wonderful thing about the huge engine was its whistle. A long, shrill blast echoing through the woods signalled Uncle's arrival while he was still half a mile away. It was a distinctive sound, too, completely different from that made by the whistle of any other rig. Uncle had equipped his steamer with a special double-toned whistle, very clear and melodic, which he had invented and built. I never heard another that sounded quite like it.

Down the road he chugged, the big steamer towing the grain separator with the spare water tank behind it. The separator was dropped between the stacks so that the feeder would be in the most convenient place for the bundle pitchers. Then the steamer was maneuvered into position. The big belt was unrolled, lifted up onto the flywheel of the engine and made taut by backing up. In a few minutes the wheels, the huge drivers of the steamer and the smaller ones on the separator, were blocked, and everything was ready.

Slowly the great belt began to move, and with a mounting roar the rig went into motion. Up to the top of the grain stacks clambered the men who were to pitch the sheaves down, and soon the yellow bundles were falling steadily into the feeder of the separator. I climbed into the wagon box and stood by the grain spout, waiting for the first dump to come down. There! The tripper up by the scale flew back and the hard slippery kernels streamed through my fingers and down into the grain tank.

But I didn't stay there long; there were too many exciting things to look into elsewhere. The fire under the boiler of the engine was fed with straw and sometimes, when the steam was up and the fire going good, the fireman could be persuaded to let me handle the fork for a few minutes. What fun it was to slip the straw down the chute and into the roaring firebox, or to watch the water man pump water into the boiler, the great belt bobbing up and down in smooth, rhythmic motion.

Up on top of the engine the governor, with its two round balls, spun round and round so fast it was nothing but a dizzy blur. From the blower of the separator poured a steady stream

of golden straw that accumulated into a large stack as the day wore on. After nightfall I loved to watch the sparks fly upward from the smokestack of the engine, jump giddily hither and thither for a moment, then fade into the black of the night.

It was a thrill to hear the different threshing rigs around the neighborhood whistle in the mornings. There was sometimes keen rivalry between the firemen as to which one could get up steam and be the first to sound the whistle. In the evenings, too, when the day's work was over, the whistles sounded their clarion, melodious calls.

During the day one could tell what was going on around a steam-powered threshing rig by the whistle, too. The code probably varied in different parts of the country, but in our neighborhood two toots meant they were running low on straw for the engine. Three was a warning to the water hauler to get back from the spring, water was needed. A series of short quick toots indicated that the grain tank by the separator was filling up, and for the grain hauler unloading by the granary to get a move on.

It was always exciting when the rig was moved, and a joy undiluted when I was allowed to ride in the straw carrier, perched more or less precariously near the huge rear wheels which turned majestically, leaving great wide tracks in the soft earth. Would the old wooden bridges spanning the creeks hold up under the weight of the heavy steamer? It was always a moot question.

And the talk around the supper table in the evenings, after it was too dark to thresh longer and the crew had come in to eat! There were stirring tales of coulee crossings, of safety plugs

What fun it was to slip the straw down the chute and into the roaring firebox, or to watch the water man pump water into the boiler, the great belt bobbing up and down in smooth, rhythmic motion.

blowing, of rivalry between threshing crews, of being stuck in wet fields or in patches of drift sand, stories that went back to the "good old days" even then.

Or it might be that from its bracket away up on the wall the kerosene lamp flickered, while down below a discussion as to the relative merits of various makes of machines moved a seesaw course. Uncle's steamer was a Buffalo Pitts, but in earlier days he had worn out one Northwestern and one Coline, for he was an old hand at the threshing game. Someone in the group would always champion the big engine because of the extra power it developed. Uncle, however, preferred a smaller machine because, being lighter, the danger of getting stuck in soft or sandy ground wasn't as great.

One by one the old steam engines wore out and were no longer replaced. Why? There were objections, especially from the womenfolk who had to do the cooking to feed the large crews necessary to operate them. Some farmers, too, felt they needed all the straw for feeding and bedding the cattle during the winters. In the steam engines' place came gasoline- and kerosene-burning engines Later the combines came on the scene.

An era had arrived when something else could do the work better and more economically, and so the steam-powered giants were crowded off the scene. But I miss them, their clear musical whistle on fall mornings, and their lusty *chuck-a-chuck-a-chuck* as they made the dust fly out of the old separators.

Steam power had the best of the gasoline engine in some ways, though it had its disadvantages, too. It was simple, for the old steamers had no gears and no clutches. But there was only one speed ahead and one in reverse, controlled by the throttle. Going from one place to another was slow work, especially if straw was used for fuel, for then the rack behind the engine had to be refilled twice or even more for each

There were many makes of grain separators, too—the Avery, the Minneapolis, the Rumely and the Red River Special being well-known in our region. They were the subjects of quite as many controversies over the coffee cups as the iron giants that provided the power.

Sometimes a group of neighbors would get together, organize a "gang" and help each other with the threshing. Then the grain was not stacked, the shocks being hauled in to the threshing machine by team and wagon. "Bundle teams" they were called, and it took 10 or 12 of them to keep the rig running steadily. Shock threshing required large crews, 20 or 25 men, all told.

mile traveled. On long moves, cordwood or soft coal was often used.

For years now I have threshed my grain with a combine. It's wonderfully efficient and, when compared with driving all over the neighborhood as part of a steam threshing crew, far easier and more convenient. But a combine hasn't any "color"; as a machine it seems prosaic and uninteresting; all it's good for is to thresh grain. I admit I wouldn't want to go back to the "Good Old Days" of steam threshing, but I concede too that there was an aura of romance about the old steam rigs. It's been years now since I've heard a steamer whistle on a frosty, clear, late fall morning. ❖

Stubble-Dragged

By Andrew Livingston

I shall never forget the night I was stubble-dragged by the crew of the threshing machine I was working on. I didn't know why they did it until the next morning, and I was pretty angry about it. I chuckle when I think of it now, but at the time it wasn't a bit funny to me.

It was one of those nights when the harvest moon hung in the sky like a great lantern. The air was hushed and all around me the rolling wheat country was bathed in soft, silvery light.

I heard once, somewhere, if you slept in the moonlight you would get moon madness. I'm not superstitious, but I chose a spot around the big straw stack that was in shadow.

I raked out a place in the loose straw and spread my bed. Then, pulling off my shoes, I rolled up in my blankets.

We who worked on the machine traveled with it and lived with it as we moved from farm to farm. We had a cook wagon where we ate our meals and where Mrs. Robinson and Mrs. Hartung did the cooking. At night, we slept around the straw stacks.

Half-drowsy, I could hear the other fellows in the crew down by the big tractor or steam engine. Usually they all rolled in when I did, but tonight I suspected there was some mischief afoot. But I didn't dream it involved me.

I was 20 years old and I had been married only a week when Fred Wilson asked me if I'd come to work for him. My father-in-law loaned me one of his teams and I was all set to make a nice chunk of money for us to start house-keeping on.

I made $6 a day just to make one trip a day to town with the team and wagon to get a load of coal for the engine. The field pitchers earned $3.50 a day and the other men $4, so that made me sort of an aristocrat around the rig.

I was lying there drowsily looking up at the stars and dreaming of when the harvest would be over and I could go home to my bride. I heard footsteps running around the stack, and the next minute I could see a bunch of men outlined against the sky. Someone said in a low voice, "Is this him?" And somebody else said, "It's him, all right."

Before I could move or yell, they grabbed my blankets at the foot and started hauling me out across the stubble. I kept still until I could see what was going to happen next.

We reached the tracks where the wagons had been coming into the thresher when an oncoming car swung its headlights toward us. The men dropped the ends of the blankets and ran back. I jumped to my feet and, gathering up my blankets in my arms, I started to get out of the way of that car, but he veered off and circled me.

When I got back to the straw stack, all was quiet. Every man was rolled in his blankets, and some were even snoring. I knew they weren't asleep, but I decided to wait until morning. I was pretty mad about the whole thing.

The next morning when I went to the cook wagon, I was purposely a little late. There were big grins on the faces of everyone there except the women.

It was Fred Wilson who let the cat out of the bag.

"I see you got stubble-dragged last night," he said with a chuckle. "That happens to all new married men. You sure got out of the road when you thought I was going to run over you."

At that, everyone roared and the two women, who had been looking mystified, joined in.

So that was my initiation. At first I was hot with embarrassment; then I began to get angry, but looking at the faces of those men I couldn't stay that way. They were my friends.

"Just you wait," I said threateningly, "until one of you gets married." I joined in the roar that followed. ❖

Woodcutting

By Onalee Lytle Hoffman

Putting up wood in the old days was a way of life. It wasn't an alternative to supplement some form of oil, gas or electric heat as is the trend today.

Looking back to the priorities of childhood, we probably didn't appreciate the authenticity of that old Warm Morning kitchen range that cooked the tough old hen all day for noodles. We merely observed the golden loaves of bread and cinnamon rolls that came from it. We certainly didn't appreciate packing out of the ashes and getting scolded for not putting them into the bucket carefully so as not to have ash dust in everything from the bed blankets to the drinking-water pail.

My dad was one of those people who never prepared for winter. It was seldom in my childhood years that a pile of wood cut stove-length was ready when winter threatened her first onslaught.

Mother saw that the work got done. On Saturdays in early fall she would send Mary Ann, my oldest sister, and me out to gather wood. We'd take the huge old hayrack and team, spending several hours to load it high. I often wondered how we lifted great logs up when we were young.

By late fall we would have two great piles ready for Dad to saw. It had to be piled so the smaller wood for the kitchen stove was on one side, and the logs and bigger branches on the other side to make sawing easier for Dad, but somehow he never got around to starting the old balky tractor and buzz saw. The buzz saw was run from the momentum of a huge canvas belt that slipped around the flywheel on the tractor. When the

It was seldom in my childhood years that a pile of wood cut stove-length was ready when winter threatened her first onslaught.

dead of winter had settled in, there was no way of starting one of those old cold-blooded Twin City tractors. There was one alternative though. You guessed it—saw the wood with the crosscut saw. We kids knew what the first chore was when we came from school.

Seemed I was always on one end of the crosscut with either Lyla, my older sister, or Joe, the brother just younger than me. You know what happened to a crosscut saw when it wasn't pulled straight and clean through the cut? Well, it stuck, that's what.Then we'd laugh like crazy as we attempted to yank the thing out of a half-sawed log.

When Mother didn't hear the thud of wood on the porch in due time, she knew what was going on. She would show up at the door with a shout. "Stop your nonsense and get that wood cut before dark!"

Our mother never had much of a sense of humor; we never fooled her any. In those years with the meager outer clothes available, we were next to frozen. No sympathy—just get the wood in. As soon as she closed the door, we made that old saw really hum so we could get the wood in, do our barn chores and milking before we froze to death or before dark, whichever came first.

One winter, along about 1942, we kids were relieved of our daily after-school task of sawing

wood. Our oldest brother, Jack, showed up off the Russ Madison Rodeo Circuit. He borrowed the neighbor's tractor in agreement to furnish him his winter's wood for the use of it. He hauled in several more loads before starting a day of sawing.

How Dad complained when Jack gave so much wood to the neighbor! His complaining turned to sudden fear at the near end of sawing. Cottonwood could be tricky, as often a limb could be hollow or have a punky center, but give no indication on the outside. The saw caught the punk, pulling Jack's arm into the saw instantly. His arm was gashed open deeply from just below his thumb to the point of his elbow. It was a mean, jagged wound. Being a bronc rider and having been hurt quite seriously many times, he kept himself calm in the face of Dad's near-hysteria.

Mother wrapped his arm in a clean sheet and hurried him into the old car. Dad drove the 50 miles to the doctor in Rapid City, S.D. Jack snickered, "Scared heck out of Dad; he drove old jitney 50 miles an hour." He had never driven it over 20 miles an hour since he had owned the Buick, as it didn't have any brakes.

Those were the old "have-to" woodcutting, wood-burning days. We still use a Home Comfort wood kitchen range. It fries meat beautifully, simmers the soup all day.

Modern times have changed; many do heat their homes partially or completely with draft-controlled wood heating units. Wood is hauled home with pickups and trailers. It is common for an entire family to go on a woodcutting outing on weekends. Children gladly exchange Saturday's cartoons on TV for a wood-getting excursion in the great out-of-doors. ❖

Making Sorghum Molasses

By Garnet Quiett

I can still remember the taste of sorghum molasses served with hot, homemade biscuits and freshly churned butter when I was a child.

We lived on a farm in Central Texas. We grew most of our food, buying only such staples as flour, sugar, K.C. baking powder, salt, Arm and Hammer soda, coffee beans, and peanut oil.

My father planted an acre or two of sorghum cane to make molasses. The juice in this cane was sweet and the stalks very juicy. He also planted a small patch near the hog pens to feed the hogs. My two younger sisters and I would break off several stalks and climb the rail fence enclosing the pens, sit on the top rail and chew the juicy joints of cane. We would throw some stalks into the pens for the hogs to eat, as it amused us to see them eating the cane.

In late summer, when the sorghum cane reached ripeness, it was harvested. My father and brother made stripping knives by whittling one edge of a barrel stave thinner than the other. Then they whittled a handle on one end. We used these to strip the leaves off the stalks.

My sisters and I walked between the rows of cane and stripped the leaves from the stalks. My younger sister, Gay, and I were too small to strip the leaves off the tops of the stalks, so we stripped off some of the lower leaves.

When we had finished stripping the leaves off the cane stalks, our father would cut the stalks and pile them.

After the stalks were cut and piled, Father hitched the mules to the wagon and he and my brother loaded the piles of cane onto it and hauled it to the sorghum mill.

Our neighbor Mr. Slaughter had a sorghum mill and made molasses for people who brought him their sorghum cane. Once I begged my father to let Gay and me go to the mill with him. I was fascinated by the strange procedure which turned the cane into thick, sweet molasses.

The sorghum mill consisted of a brick kiln fired by a log fire under it. The cooking pan had a copper bottom which fit the top of the furnace.

Mr. Slaughter fed the cane stalks into a crusher, which was two big steel rollers in a frame. The power was a horse or mule hitched to a long shaft connected to the crusher. The animal pulled this shaft around and around, turning the steel rollers.

We kids had a ball playing around the sorghum mill and generally getting in the way. Mr. Slaughter threatened to send us to the house if we didn't stay out of the way, but he never did.

As the first pouring of juice was being put into containers, we whittled spoons from cane stalks and ate the foam.

The juice ran from the crusher down troughs into a cooking vat, where it cooked until the water was cooked out of it. As the juice cooked, a skim formed which had to be taken off. One or two men would skim the molasses and put the skim into a skimming hole, a pit dug beside the furnace.

Mildred, one of the Slaughter kids, had the misfortune of falling into the skimming pit. Her mother took her to a stock tank nearby and washed her off. From then on, she was careful to veer around the skimming pit!

When the first cooking of molasses was done, a stopper was pulled out of the vat and the thick molasses ran down a trough into a pot. It was dipped out and put into gallon buckets or small wooden kegs. The aroma from the molasses was so delicious!

Just before sundown, we were ready to go home. Our kegs of molasses were loaded on the wagon. When we got home, my father put the kegs in the cellar. He placed one keg on a V-shaped wooden horse. It was a simple matter to pull the stopper and draw a bucket of molasses as needed for table use.

I remember that when the kegs were empty, they were stored in the smokehouse. In the summer, we kids would fish the sticky, white residue which the remaining molasses had become out of the kegs and chew it like chewing gum. We called it "sweet gum."

Never have I found sorghum molasses which could match the taste of Mr. Slaughter's molasses! ✛

Sorghum-Cooking Time

By Iola E. Miller

At the end of the tobacco harvest, there was a chore that quite a few farmers of yesterday had to do—harvesting the sugarcane and cooking the juice into golden-brown syrup or molasses. There are a few farmers who still pursue the art today.

Many times several neighbors would join together and cook all day and into the night. This became a fun time for many, but it was only for those who knew the art. It was not only fun, but very dangerous, as I will relate.

In late September the leaves were stripped from the cane by a downstroke with a special stick, leaving the cane bare and clear of the fodder, or leaves. The cane heads were cut and saved for feed, the birds, and sometimes the hogs. The stalks were cut and hauled by wagon to the cane press which had been set up.

Mike, our mule, was hitched to the end of a long pole attached to the press. Mike was made to travel in a wide circle, making the press turn. The boys took turns feeding the stalks of cane between two big corrugated discs of steel which pressed out the juice into a huge pail.

This was the dangerous job. When Mike circled, the one feeding the press would "duck" for the pole to pass overhead. Once a brother of mine failed to duck quickly enough and his head was caught between the pole and the press, resulting in a very painful injury.

The men were busy at the big cooking pan, which was about 10 feet long and about 4 feet wide, sectioned off into areas about 6 inches wide, closed at one end and opened at the other, so that as the juice cooked, it traveled back and forth. The pan was set on a foundation so that a fire could be built under it.

The juice was removed with a long-handled scoop. As the cooking progressed more juice was added. The liquid thickened and turned color. The big pan had to be kept full at all times. When the cooker decided that the sap was done, he opened the plug on the far end and started the thick brown liquid running through the hole and into large pails. From there it was funneled into wooden kegs or barrels.

The press was then cleaned. The scum was poured into a deep hole in the ground and covered completely to prevent anyone or anything from walking into it, as the scum was hot and sticky for several hours, even on cool nights.

If you have never tasted hot biscuits and butter spread with new, warm, homemade molasses, you have missed one of the better things of life. I also loved my mother's sorghum puddings. I am delighted to share the sorghum pudding recipe with you and hope each of you will enjoy it. ❖

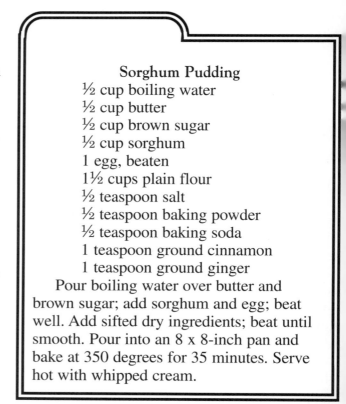

Sorghum Pudding
½ cup boiling water
½ cup butter
½ cup brown sugar
½ cup sorghum
1 egg, beaten
1½ cups plain flour
½ teaspoon salt
½ teaspoon baking powder
½ teaspoon baking soda
1 teaspoon ground cinnamon
1 teaspoon ground ginger

Pour boiling water over butter and brown sugar; add sorghum and egg; beat well. Add sifted dry ingredients; beat until smooth. Pour into an 8 x 8-inch pan and bake at 350 degrees for 35 minutes. Serve hot with whipped cream.

Harvesttime

By W.E. Albertson

I always get a thrill at the sight of a huge combine plowing its way across a field of ripe grain, the huge reel gently nudging the heads of wheat or rice back to the machine which will thresh them, separating the golden yellow kernels from the straw, then spraying the straw back to the ground from whence it came.

It was not always like this. My mind goes back to the year 1918. Harvesttime, back then, was a slow and tedious process. The men who cut the wheat were known as harvest hands, a motley crew coming from here, there and everywhere. They rode in on freight trains. The railroad cops just looked the other way and let them ride free. The railroad needed the wheat—a big source of revenue.

I was a harvest hand myself, although I never rode a freight. My favorite brother, Ed, was farming the old home farm not far from Wichita and was glad to have me (Bud, as he called me) to help cut the wheat. The grain ripened in early June. The waving field was losing the last trace of green and had turned to the characteristic yellow-gold of ripened wheat.

Ed rigged the binder to be pulled by his tractor instead of horses. I drove the tractor with a Mr. Taylor riding and operating the binder. The binder was only 7 feet wide, a far cry from the modern combine which cuts a swath of 25 feet or more. Today's combines have air-conditioned cabs and two-way radios. We had only a big straw hat to protect us from the blazing sun, with temperatures of 100 degrees and more, and the tractor belching heat and fumes into our faces.

The binder cut the wheat and tied it into bundles which would later be stacked into shocks, then later, at threshing time, hauled in "bundle wagons" to a threshing machine which separated the grain from the straw. The straw was not returned to the ground but stood in great stacks which were of little or no use. Cattle would eat some of the straw during the winter when forage was scarce.

It took two long, hard days to cut the south 40 acres, and we thought we were doing pretty well for that day and time. Now a modern combine would cut the whole field in a few hours.

After harvest, I stayed on to help Ed with the plowing. I drove five horses abreast hitched to a riding plow. The plow turned 24 inches of sod as it went.

One day at noon I stopped the horses and drove them to the barn for their dinner. When I returned, I drove them into place and was getting ready to hitch up when a bumblebee came at me from under the plow. There was a nest of the big wild bees there.

I left the scene as quickly as I could. I knew the power of those bees; unlike a honeybee which stings only once, the bumblebee just keeps on stinging time after time. I was wearing a denim jacket and the bee stung me through the jacket right between the shoulders. I got out of that jacket fast.

I had a problem. If the bees stung the horses, they would panic and run away, creating havoc in every direction. When horses panic, they go berserk. They will tear the harness to shreds or run through wire fences, sometimes cutting themselves badly.

Bees always have a sentry which guards the nest. Apparently it was the sentry which stung me, for as I maneuvered the horses away from the area, not another bee came out. Luck was on my side. I managed to get the horses away from the bees' nest and hitch them to the plow without further incident. It was a good day for me. ✣

Mama's Feather Beds

By Fay Frye Vangilder

One of the good things about the good old days was the feather bed. In fact, in retrospection, the method by which the feathers for the beds were obtained is also pleasant to remember. Farming in the good old days was not so specialized as it is today and since my father grain-farmed several acres of the old Bee Hunter Marsh, many head of horses were necessarily kept for this work, usually some six or eight teams. But the horses were not the only animals important to farm life.

It took a variety of animals, great and small, to round out farm life, and they were very essential to help make the farm pay in order that farmers might earn their living. The horses were, of course, the greatest animals in size on our farm and I would have to think a spell to recall exactly which was the smallest, but somewhere in between the great and the small was the old gray goose!

It took a variety of animals, great and small, to round out farm life, and they were very essential to help make the farm pay.

Mama was a great one for trying new breeds, especially of chickens. Inevitably a new breed of chicken would show up at our farm. "Just a few, until we see how they will do. Who knows? These may be the best layers yet," Mama always said.

Not so with the geese. Once Mama decided she was going to raise geese. She sent for all the catalogs which specialized in geese only. These she studied very carefully until she came to a decision. The big gray Toulouse had the honor of being chosen, and retained that honor at our farm for as long as Mama raised geese.

That first order of eggs became the beginning of a flock of geese which was continued until there was a feather bed for every bed in the house and for every child in the family. When the first eggs arrived, Mama was ready. She had insured her success at the starting gate by making certain there were enough hens in the setting notion to take care of the eggs.

Of course, there were trials and tribulations a-plenty, but farming was then and still is one great long gamble.

One of the problems, as I recall, was that a hen might tire of setting the four-week period required to hatch the goose eggs when her natural instinct told her she should have had baby chicks after three weeks. When his happened I saw Mama, if necessary, practically force a hen to set figuratively. Literally, she worked very patiently at gentle persuasion, helping the reluctant hen make up her mind to continue the setting.

Another serious and sometimes fatal problem was caused by early spring rains, when the little goslings wanted to run out in the rain and the mother hen disagreed, but would nevertheless sit sadly in the cold rain, trying to persuade the goslings to hover. Ridiculous as it may seem, the goslings, after becoming chilled, would stand with their heads up, water running off their backs or down their necks until they literally chilled or drowned (as we then said), unless we gathered them into baskets, wrapped them in cloth and put them in a warm place—usually behind the stove.

The most frustrating of all for the foster mother was when the goslings decided to go for a swim in the creek. When this happened, all Mother Hen could do was run frantically along the edge of the stream, alternately squawking and clucking, until in prostration, she gave up and wandered off to pick at the grass and call feebly to her brood from time to time.

Through all this Mama persevered until she had a flock of geese large enough to take care of the goslings without the aid of the hen mothers. After that, the only part the hens played in the roll of geese raising was to aid in the hatching.

Once Mama had determined the size of the flock, this number—some 25 or 30 geese, along with the proper number of ganders to insure a high percent of fertility—was maintained throughout the long years until Mama reached her goal. A part of this goal, I might add, was

the family tradition to have for each child a wedding gift a feather bed, and we were four daughters.

Twice each summer we had goose-picking day, the first of which came early in July. The exact time of picking, however, depended upon the time of hatching, which in turn was affected by the spring weather. Sometimes the spring flock was not mature enough for the first picking, but the old ones always got it.

Once the young had matured enough that they were considered safe from predators, the entire flock was put out to pasture. This meant they were allowed to spend the blissful summer days snipping tender blades of grass, roaming over the lush pasture-land which was shared by a number of horses and several milk cows. They drank from the stream which flowed across the southeast corner of the pasture, and swam and dipped and bathed in the pond. Together they could scream and hiss and flail any assailant that might have decided to descend upon them.

Sometimes during a very dry summer when ponds and streams dried up, the pesky geese would get into the water trough. When this happened, Papa and the farmhands would come in for dinner at high noon, both men and horses hot, tired, and thirsty, only to find the horses would not drink the water. The dirty water had to be dumped and the trough refilled.

Mama's beautiful flock of Toulouse geese, oblivious to all the problems, spent the summer days in blissful, lazy idleness, growing feathers and getting fat grazing in the bluegrass. Always at twilight they could be seen slowly eating their way toward the safety of the barnyard for a night's repose after they had been tossed a limited amount of grain for dessert and as an enticement to come in at night.

At the crack of dawn, their heads came out from under their wings, they stretched their long graceful necks, flapped their wings, let out a few piercing screams, and headed for the green pastures long before other animals, including man, were astir—except on goose-picking days. This day they found the gate to the pasture securely closed and themselves fastened in the dusty barnyard.

The horse stalls on one side of the barn had been thoroughly cleaned the day before and filled with clean straw. After the morning chores were completed, Mama gathered the large, 25-pound paper flour sacks which she had been saving since the previous summer, plus a handful of string made by tearing strips from worn-out clothing, and a comfortable straight-backed chair from the back porch and headed for the barn. Goose picking was about to begin!

I was usually the one who went with Mama to catch the geese. I suppose this was because I was skinny, long-limbed, swift of foot and quick on the trigger. Also, I wasn't afraid of those old geese. We corralled the flock into the clean stalls, Mama's chair was carefully placed, the paper flour sack was secured, the first goose caught and we were in business.

Mama always cut the feet off a pair of the long black stockings which had been worn

At the crack of dawn, they headed for the green pastures long before other animals, including man—were astir, except on goose-picking days.

during the winter, sewed them across the cut end, then cut finger holes, thus making herself a pair of long stocking gloves which reached to the dress sleeves where they were pinned with safety pins. This left her fingers free for picking and protected her arms from being sharply nipped by an irate goose who did not appreciate having its feathers plucked.

Once the geese were in the confines of the stalls, they were not too hard to catch except they had to be caught a certain way, usually by the neck, to avoid injury to the goose. Also, the wings had to be held down just to avoid injury to the catcher. Most of our animals were not too wild as they were all gently treated.

Mama covered her lap with an old dress or shirt, took the goose with her left hand and held it by the legs, breast up, while at the same time she tucked its neck under her left arm. This freed her right hand for picking. This

plucking worried me until Mama assured me that it did not hurt the goose, if properly done. Evidently she was right, because after the shock of the first few plucks, they offered little or no resistance.

First, the best, most downy breast feathers were taken up to the base of the neck, then the downy ones on the back, again to the base of the long neck and from around the wings. Mama was careful not to remove certain feathers from under each wing so that the wings could stay in place; Mama always said so they wouldn't slide down. There was a real knack to this, and Mama seldom made a mistake.

The perplexed goose was then set free in the barnyard where it wandered about in bewilderment at its nakedness and aloneness until it was soon joined by the next victim. This continued until the entire flock was picked with Mama and me stopping just long enough for dinner. Sometimes it took two days, in which case the geese were turned out of the stalls at night, and given grain, but kept in the barnyard.

As one sack was filled, Mama would tie it carefully with the rag string before placing it in a safe place. Mama never allowed me to pick a goose although I asked to try once just to see if I could. The feathers soon grew back so that the second picking always came before school began in the fall, and early enough that the geese would be fully feathered and ready for the chilly winds of early autumn. Six flour sacks a summer was considered a good season's crop. This went on year after year until Mama reached her goal.

And the beds! I think perhaps the nearest thing to heaven that a child could ever know was snuggling down into the deep bed of feathers after a climb up the long stairs to a very cold room. To sleep the long winter night through was literally like drifting and dreaming on a cloud.

We all got our feather beds and still have them. They were indeed gifts representative of the true labor of love. Yes, Mama was some goose picker! ✤

Apple Business

By Ann Baumgard

Life on the farm wasn't easy when I was a little girl, but there were occasions which made work a pleasure. The only real convenience we had was electric lighting. We had no power washing machine, no mixer, refrigerator, hot water heater, lawn mower, electric stove, coffeepot nor any other appliance.

Everything was done by hand. Ma's washer worked by pushing a lever back and forth by hand. It wasn't such a bad job, for my sister Mat and I would pull and push the lever together, singing ridiculous songs such as:

"Strawberry shortcake, huckleberry pie
V-I-C-T-O-R-Y
Are we in it? Well, I guess,
Good old wash machine, yes, yes, yes."

Cakes, sauces and batters were stirred by hand.

An old icebox stood in the kitchen, with a pan sitting under it which constantly overflowed from melting ice. Uncle August and Pa cut ice blocks on the river in midwinter and stored them in a special shed. Sawdust buried each block and it was remarkable how the ice remained stone hard all summer. Whenever Mat and I got a chance on a hot day, we'd sneak into the shed and hack off a chunk and suck on it to cool off.

No one on the farm ever cut the lawn, for there was always a sheep or two running around, cropping the grass as it grew.

In the kitchen, Ma had a large wood-burning stove with a reservoir attached. It was Mat's and my job to keep the woodbox and reservoir filled so we always had heat and warm water. In the front room was a wood-burning stove. We two kids staggered as we carried in big, long-lasting chunks and stacked them behind the stove.

A large gray granite coffeepot sat on the stove, ever ready to provide a cup of hot coffee to whoever came into the kitchen. Every so often,

> *In the kitchen, Ma had a large wood-burning stove. It was Mat's and my job to keep the woodbox and reservoir filled so we always had heat and warm water.*

We girls peeled. Ma did the fine work of cutting out cores, wormy spots and blemishes, and quartering the fruit. (She didn't trust either of us to do that, for Mat would be tempted to leave half a worm now and then just to see if Ma would find out, and of course I'd never tell! Trust Mat to think up crazy things to do!)

Ma would pack the apple pieces in a 2-gallon stoneware crock, filling it three-quarters full. Then she would set a little flat china sauce dish on top of the apples. On the dish she would place a piece of cotton batting about the size of a silver dollar. On it she would sprinkle 1½ teaspoons of flowers of sulphur.

"Now get ready, girls," she'd say. "I'm going to light the cotton."

We'd bring a close-fitting cover, a big piece of brown wrapping paper and some store string.

Then came the most exciting part! Ma would hold the cover ready in one hand, strike a match with the other and light the cotton. "Now look quick, girls," she'd say. "Watch the blue fire!"

When the fire had a good start on the cotton, a thick bluish-yellow cloud would come forth! The escaping cloud would set us all to coughing!

"See?" she'd say, and then would quickly set the cover on the crock. Then she'd tie brown paper around the top to keep in the fumes and set it aside to "cook" for at least three hours.

Ma would add a half-cup of fresh grounds to keep the coffee fresher-tasting. By and by the pot became too heavy with grounds and they had to be dumped out. Then the whole coffee-cooking procedure would start all over again.

Because Ma had to help in the barn, Mat and I had to help with housework when chores were done. We became quite adept with sharp knives.

Everything prepared for cooking—meat, fruit or vegetables—had to be cut up by hand. I recall apple paring, especially during harvesting of the various varieties. Besides making applesauce, Ma dried apples and also sulphured many gallons of the fruit. The earliest varieties, Yellow Transparent, Duchess and St. Lawrence, were sulphured because they were rather delicately fleshed and could not endure the drying process very well.

Pa would pick the apples just before they were primely ripe. Then Ma, Mat and I had to get going.

She always used the same recipe—1½ gallons of prepared apples, 1½ teaspoons of flowers of sulphur. Cover tightly and let apples sit in fumes for three hours or longer.

Usually the next morning she would put the snow-white, treated apples in quart Mason jars and label them "Sulphured Apples. Be sure to rinse well before using."

How good they were in pies, kuchen, fritters and apple betty.

Drying apples was a different experience. This came in early fall. Pewaukees, Greenings and Grimes Goldens were for drying. Snow apples were stored for eating.

way and set aside the pieces that were crooked or too small. She used only the perfect ones for drying. The imperfect pieces were to be dealt with later, so they were dropped into cold salted water to keep them from discoloring.

Now came the second step. Ma washed the oilcloth on the kitchen table for the "umpteenth" time and laid the slices in even rows on it. Then she'd get her frycake cutter and go over each slice. A hard push and the core would be cut out. Now do you understand why the slices had to be well chosen?

At just the proper time, Pa would pick the apples and bring them into the kitchen.

"Come on, girls, these apples aren't getting any younger," Ma would call, and we'd respond eagerly, for this was a job we liked.

Apples for drying were chosen carefully according to size. They had to be just right to fit Ma's doughnut cutter.

Ma would wash them. Mat and I would peel and Ma would slice them into uniform slices. "Show us the star," I'd say, and Ma would cut the first apple in half crosswise, not from top to bottom through the stem.

"See, God puts the star of Bethlehem in every apple. Each seed or pair of seeds sleeps in a little cradle like the Christ Child did," Ma would say. (Dear reader, try it sometime. Cut an apple through the middle and you'll see what Ma showed us.)

That bit of humble lore set the pace, for we were serious for at least 10 minutes, and peeled seriously. Ma would slice the apples the round

Then she'd carefully string the sliced rings on a clean, stout piece of twine. She'd hang the strung slices across the corner of the kitchen above the stove, carefully separate the rings on the string, drape a piece of clean mosquito netting over all and the job was done.

Now all we had to do was to wait about a week and the slices would be dry enough to store.

Mat and I would pick up the core pieces and seeds and save them for the chickens. Then Mat and I were given the kettle of discarded pieces and slices to fix for applesauce. We had to cut away core sections, bits of peeling and bruises.

"Remember, no worms, or there'll be no sauce."

The irregularly shaped hunks of apple were soon simmering on the back of the stove. Ma would drop in enough sugar to taste and sauce would soon be ready for supper.

Somehow, the applesauce I make today doesn't have the flavor of Ma's. ❖

Razorback Roundup

By Arthur E. Williams

Back in the early days when a roundup was mentioned, you immediately thought of large herds of cattle banded together to be driven to market, but it's not the cattle roundup I am going to tell you about today. It's a roundup all right, but one that you have probably never read about, or even heard of. It's the Razorback Roundup.

Seventy years ago I was a 6-year-old boy, and I can remember as clearly as if it were yesterday when it was Razorback Roundup time.

My dad had several hundred head of hogs on the free range of the Devil's Pocket. This land was dense with underbrush, briar patches, canebrakes, and creeks and lakes full of alligators. These 'gators caught many hogs as they came to the creeks to drink water.

In the Pocket, there were high ridges, and they were very thickly covered with different kinds of oak trees which produced acorns in abundance. When the acorns began to fall, the hogs became fat, and it was time for the Razorback Roundup.

Razorback was a name given to the native hogs that ran the open range. In the summer the hogs rooted up roots to sustain them. During this time they were struggling to survive, they became very poor. Their backs showed like a razor's edge, hence the name, Razorback.

We always kept track of our hogs. We went out into the swamps with our hog dogs. The dogs would find them and round them up and keep them in a bunch until Dad and I came to them. Dad always carried some corn in a bag thrown over his shoulder. He would shell some of this corn and feed the hogs, and in this way kept them about half gentle.

In the spring when the pigs were small, we made pens out in the Pocket and penned them. We marked the pigs and castrated the male pigs so they would make better meat.

In the fall, after the hogs were fat on acorns, we rounded them up, penned them and cut out all the ones we wanted to sell. Then we put the ones we were going to sell in small pens so they wouldn't have room for much exercise.

We had no trucks to haul our hogs to market. We drove them just like they did the cattle, and driving 103 half-wild hogs 12 miles is no small task.

I remember the first drive I made with Dad and some of the neighbors. We drove these hogs 12 miles to market. They were fat and we had to let them go slow.

When we got to the market pens, Dad and the buyer picked two that they thought were average. Then they weighed these two and the two averaged 175 pounds, so that is what they decided was the weight of each hog. Do you know what we got paid for these fat hogs, delivered? Three cents a pound! I will never forget as I watched the buyer pay Dad in cash. He counted out $540.75. I didn't know that there was that much money in the world!

Then we went to the general store. Dad bought some cheese and crackers and a bottle of soda pop for me, the first one I had ever had.

When we reached home that night, after having ridden 24 miles, I was dead tired. It had been quite a day for a 6-year-old, but before I went to sleep that night, all I could see was the buyer counting out all that money to Dad. As I drifted off into the land of dreams, I could only see the future, when I would have all this money counted out to me. ❖

> *In the fall, after the hogs were fat on acorns, we rounded them up, penned them and cut out all the ones we wanted to sell.*

Down Row

By Miz Ackerman

When the first hint of fall comes, the trees parade their new fall wardrobe; geese go sailing, honking their contempt for mere mortals who have to stay on the ground and work for a living; and my thoughts turn to corn gathering and the "down row." I am convinced that Womens' Lib is the afterbirth of the down row.

For those of you who have never gathered corn and are asking what the down row is, let me explain. If you had a bad hay crop and you needed extra fodder to help get the stock through the winter, you cut and shocked the cornstalks and came back later to shuck out the

ears of corn and retie the bundles of fodder. This wasn't too bad; you could set your own pace and dream a little along the way—how you were going to leave the farm and make your fortune and never have to work in the fields again, little realizing you would soon reverse your dream and long to be back where you started, down on the farm.

But, if your hay crop was good, you gathered your corn from the field. Counting off five rows, you drove the team to straddle the middle row, thus the down row.

For those of you who don't know the trials and tribulations of the down row, lend your ear. If you had a good team (the Ackermans were famous for theirs), you wrapped the reins around the knob on the headboard of the wagon box. Then, with a few *gees* and *haws*, you controlled your team—well, almost controlled them. They immediately began to bite off, bite at, slobber on or wallow in their mouth every ear of corn in reach in an attempt to chew it, which they were unable to do because of the bits in their mouths. So down it would go under the wagon among the saw

briers and cockleburrs to be shucked by the one who gathered the down row. To add insult to injury, we had a built-in fertilizing process going on at the same time. The team would chomp and stomp and whish their tails all in one operation, or so it seemed.

Now if two of us went to the field, we each took two rows on either side of the wagon and our half of the down row. I was slower than my husband, so he usually had more than his share to do. If we took the twins to the field with us, we gave them the down row, and this wasn't too bad, but with only the twins in the field with my husband, the idea somehow came into being that the daughter, Jean, being a girl, would have the best deal if she took the down row. When she was 8, I decided to leave the farm and take a job in the factory, so for eight years, guess who had the down row?

Scoot over, women libbers—in this corner, dressed in ragged overalls and a straw hat, wearing no gloves (because they were a luxury we couldn't afford), stands Jean, ex-champion of the down row. ✣

Prairie Fire!

By Daisy Proffitt Messick

When I was a child in northeastern New Mexico in the early 1900s, one of the most feared things in the lives of ranchers and homesteaders was the cry "Prairie fire!" Before the snows came, the yellow prairies were a torch waiting to be lighted. The smallest child knew the fear of the distant spiral of smoke rising into the sky and sweeping down, sometimes as fast as a horse could run.

I lived on a large ranch in Union County, and no one feared the great fires that swept the ranges more than I did. Although most well-operated, established ranches were protected by well-plowed cattle guards, sometimes a luckless homesteader's shack was caught in the path of the fire and left a pitiful skeleton on the prairie.

One bitter morning in early November of 1916, my stubborn, elderly donkey, Dick, and I had started our daily trip to the little one-room school of Cottonwood, five miles distant.

I had to pull and tug to shut the barbed-wire gate that led out of the house pasture. (My father always said that he made these gates "to keep people out and cattle in," and my small arms made very hard work of opening and shutting them.)

Suddenly a puff of west wind brought a familiar acrid whiff to my nostrils. Dick woke up and, rearing back, nearly pulled the bridle reins from my hand. Alarmed, I scanned the icy blueness above. Sure enough, there it was! To the west, beyond the rise of pasture, a high blue column plumed into the sky.

With fingers suddenly grown swift and agile, I fastened the tight, stiff gate, jumped for the saddle and raced home.

I threw down the reins and burst into the ranch kitchen where my mother was washing dishes.

"Prairie fire!" I gasped. She ran to the front porch with me, and we could see the high menacing cloud moving toward the pasture.

"The men have already gone to move cattle on the Bayne place," she cried. "Stay with your brother while I get the horses and bulls out of the pasture." She ran out the front gate across the water lot and began to whistle for her horse.

We could not hear Mother now, but we knew she was still calling Dandy, cajoling him with soft whistlings and calls, wheedling and coaxing, trying to keep her calls low and calm.

Brother and I watched from the front yard as Mother slowed her pace so as not to frighten the horses. However, each time she would reach toward Dandy, he would prance stiffly away as if playing a game. In cold weather when he was feeling frisky, he sometimes did this; then if she turned her back and walked away, he would follow her.

She tried this strategy now, and it worked. Dandy followed Mother, and the rest of the horses followed Dandy just inside the water lot.

Before she could move quickly enough to slam the big wooden gate, Traveller, a big salty blue roan, shied and broke back, just as Brother and I were exulting, "She's got 'em now!"

Brother sobbed beside me, "Mama's going to get burned up! Mama's going to get burned up!"

We could not hear Mother now, but we knew she was still calling Dandy, cajoling him with soft whistlings and calls, wheedling and coaxing, trying to keep her calls low and calm.

The fire raced closer. We saw several long-eared, lanky jack rabbits break from the high grass and flee before it. A cloud of the small, gray wheat birds that always wintered in the sunflower stalks along the creek whirred upward and fluttered into the smoky sky. The dried cattails, crisping panicles of wild millet and fluffy tufts of asters began to burst into flame. We could hear a rushing, crackling sound.

Brother was crying and I grasped the sharp pickets of the fence until blood seeped from my fingers. Our Sunday-school teacher, Mrs. Smith, had told us to pray for help in time of trouble, and I tried to pray for Mother, but all I could think of was *Now I lay me down to sleep* and that didn't seem very helpful!

Then two scared little ranch kids witnessed what I still think of as some kind of prairie miracle! Suddenly the horses broke into a gallop, whirled back toward Mother and stopped like a swirl of swallows arrested in flight. Dandy pranced up to Mother and allowed her to catch him. She flung her apron about his neck for a bridle, swung to his back and rode like the wind to round up the horses and bulls.

Once started, the horses raced for the corral, but the bulls milled nervously. Running belly to the ground, dodging and darting like the seasoned cow horse we had never known him to be, Dandy forced the bulls into a run, tails flying, horns tossing.

Clinging to Dandy's neck, her long, pink gingham skirts billowing behind her, yelling and riding in a dead run, Mother brought horses, bulls, Dandy and herself across the creek and through the high grass only seconds before the wind veered slightly and gusted the sweeping flames down across the pasture. Now the dry tules and sere marsh weeds were exploding into a high feathering ring of flame, circling the death trap from which both livestock and Mother had just escaped.

By this time my father and the ranch hands had seen the smoke and dashed in on their lathered horses. Neighbors came to help fight the fire. They came on horseback, in wagons, surreys and Model-T Fords. Nobody came on foot; we didn't have any neighbors that close. The men fought with wet gunnysacks, washtubs of water from the big horse tanks and back fires, but fanned by a rising wind, the fire roared on.

Hours later the tired firefighters straggled back, lips cracked and bleeding, faces blackened and blistered, to tell us that the fire had been stopped at the edges of the Malpias brakes several miles distant after heavily damaging our winter ranges.

When my father started inquiring about the source of this fire, he found that the small son of a homesteader, while walking across the ranch pasture to school, had, on that bitter morning, started "just a little fire in the grass to warm my hands." That little fire certainly turned quickly into a big one. When the father learned what his son had done, I think the little boy was warm enough!

Gutsy little Dandy's bones have whitened on the range of the J-J for many winters, and the tall grasses and the Indian paintbrush have waved above them for many summers. Mother is gone too, now, and I wonder how many of those who knew her in her later years as a frail, little old lady in a wheelchair could envision her as that black-haired, slender girl who made that wild and dangerous ride of long ago. ❖

Old Roan Was a Roamer

By Sylvia Brandt

Sometimes when I sit reminiscing, I think our children have missed much that is good in life. Simple pleasures we knew on the farm are far removed from our modern world.

We were the children of God-fearing, struggling farmers. It seemed then that life was one day after another of back-breaking labor. Most of our food came from the crops, livestock, and orchards. Among the stock were three milk cows. Two were ordinary domesticated animals, but one was a huge, roan Jersey with a very restless disposition.

The other two cows came home to be milked, but Old Roan was missing. Father and I went to hunt for her. Sure enough, on the far side of the pasture we found a section of fence down. We followed her tracks to the river bank, and there she was, mired down in the soft river mud, rolling her eyes and giving out with terrible moans. Father went back to the house and fetched a rope and horse, waded out in the muck and worked the line under her front legs and up over her back. He prodded and shouted while I led the horse and pulled her free and walked her home. For a few days, she was so sore she had to be coaxed to her feet to be milked.

She was back in the pasture only a day or so when a neighbor came to say he had found her in his alfalfa. She was foundered and he feared she would die.

"I doubt it," Father said, reaching for his hat. "A bolt of lightning couldn't kill her." He spent the night in the neighbor's alfalfa field nursing her by lantern light, and came home determined to get rid of her.

Late one afternoon, Mother said we should go bring the cows home. A storm was moving in. Sister and I hurried to the pasture and, alas, only two cows were there. We rushed them home. Mother and Father came in just as the rain came. When it was over, Father set out in search of Old Roan. In a short time he was back.

"Well, that old fence ripper has done it this time," he said. "Her roaming days are over. She has broken into the cane field, and I guess the lightning struck her. She's dead."

The stock was insured and the adjuster was a neighbor who lived down the road a couple of miles. Father went to see him and since it was dark by that time, he said he would get over early the next morning to appraise the cow.

Father went out early to start the chores and, lo and behold, there in the vegetable garden behind a gaping hole in the fence stood Old Roan. When Mr. Brown arrived, Father was so embarrassed Mother had to explain the situation. I still hear Mr. Brown roaring with laughter as he rode off down the road.

Father came out of the shed with hammer and staples, muttering, "Don't that just beat all? I always said even a bolt of lightning couldn't kill that old fool roan."

Mother picked up the milk pails and headed for the barn with an Irish twinkle in her eyes. ❖

Our Old Fordson Tractor

By M. Chester Nolte

When I was 10 or 11, growing up on an Iowa farm, we had horses to supply the muscle for plowing. But there was a lot of work involved in feeding, currying, harnessing and hitching six horses every day to do the fall plowing. We watched enviously as neighbor after neighbor was seen noisily turning the furrows behind a Titan or John Deere tractor.

Finally, Dad decided that if we could scrape up $300 (the cost of a stripped-down Fordson) we'd join the parade and take a chance on becoming "modern" farmers. One fall when the harvest was good, we did just that. What a proud day for the family as Dad drove the shiny vehicle briskly up the lane! Now we were keeping up with the Joneses and placing our bets on mechanical power rather than old-fashioned horsepower!

It was a new ballgame, indeed. There was good news and bad news. The bad news was that the hind (driving) wheels were shod with steel lugs that dug deep into the earth and left funny herringbone tracks in the fresh ground.

Worse yet, these powerful wheels were entirely devoid of fenders, so that the driver always had to be careful lest he lean too far in one direction and get a wake-up call from the hard steel.

One huge problem, at least for us boys, was the task of getting the brute started. There was no battery or self-starter, just a massive iron crank hanging out the front. There was a secret procedure to be followed, too. It would start only on gasoline; then when sufficiently warmed up, you could change to kerosene (which was cheaper than gas) by turning a switch.

In this way, we entered the modern machine age on the farm—but our new tractor was not at all like today's air-conditioned, radio-equipped, self-starting, enclosed powerhouses turning seven furrows at a time and even fitted with lights so plowing can go on after dark.

We would have been astounded to learn that one combine today costs more than our whole operation did in those days

The good news, of course, was that unlike horsepower, the tractor never got tired and headed for the barn. Only the stamina of the driver determined how much rich Iowa soil could be turned over in a day.

Progress has its price. No longer did we feel that, along with those sturdy draft animals, we had a partnership to subdue nature and make it yield its milk and honey.

We had cut the cord—there was no turning back. Not in our wildest dreams, however, could we imagine today's scientific, mechanical, computerized tilling of the soil.

Yet, I doubt that today's farmer, *enlightened* though he may be, can approach the heart-stopping thrill we got from learning to drive that old Fordson tractor. ❖

Apple Butter

By Pearl Adoree Franklin

An exhilarating sensation bubbled up inside me as I put the pert, white, dotted-Swiss pinafore over my school dress. My sister Maisie and I were going directly from school to our married sister's farm where Charlotte and Mother were making apple butter.

Decorum had been struggling to hold up its head until Maisie and I cleared the school. But from the vestibule, we literally exploded from the one-room Chestnut Grove school!

At the top of Tired Hill (so named by schoolmates who had to climb it going to and coming from school), we set off onto the woodsy, unused road that ended at my sister's farm. We were torn between the urge to romp though the drifts of fragrant, crisp leaves bathed in pools of late-afternoon sunshine and our haste to get to the excitement of making apple butter. The air was sweet with the odors of dying leaves, ripe fox grapes and, wafting over it all, the smell of cooking fruit.

In a small way, Maisie and I had helped to prepare for this thrilling event. We had cored apples on Sunday afternoon. Then we had taken turns enjoying the magic of the apple parer clamped to the edge of the cellar table. We would place an apple on the fork, turn the handle and marvel at the blade circling around until the whole peeling, totally intact, fell to a pan on the floor! Bushels of apples from the productive farm orchard had been gathered, sorted, cored and quartered.

At Charlotte's barn, sturdy forked poles had been cut from strong saplings driven into the earth. A third pole was laid across the two, anchored in the notches at each end. From this, a huge copper kettle hung over a fire kept at uniform heat during the long hours of cooking. Nearby was a huge woodpile. At intervals, additional cut apples and fresh cider were fed into the bubbling mass, while Mother and Charlotte shared the chores of constantly pushing, pulling and circling the long-handled apple butter paddle.

Father had used the close-grained wood of the shagbark oak for the paddle. It was made into a long, flat, perforated slat of smoothly finished wood. It measured about 6 inches wide at the bottom, tapering to the top and affixed immovably to the long handle. There must be no wobbling. This long handle permitted the stirrer to stand far enough away to prevent burns from the hot, constant fire.

After the supper dishes were washed, Maisie and I became the kettle-watchers. The red sun had long since slipped over the horizon and evening was turning cool. The pesky yellow jackets who so delighted in cut apples and cider had gone home. A light breeze was whispering a sad tale among the few remaining leaves in the maple tree. Crickets chirped among the tall grasses at the edge of scythed lawns.

As we moved in a little closer to the glowing red fire, we watched and wondered how much longer. Each tested dollop smelled done. It was shiny dark; surely this would be the last test. We nearly fell asleep. Finally, Charlotte brought out old coats for us to wear. The warmth and the dull, rhythmic sound of the paddle sent us sleepily to a nearby stack of new lumber to lie there counting the stars as they came out. We dozed; our minds were alert for the last test!

Finally, at 2 o'clock, we headed home. Maisie was carrying a lantern; I carried a basket of apples and Mother lugged a pail of hot apple butter. This was her share of this wholesome spread.

Soon we were home again. There was love and security in our house—and apple butter for breakfast. ❖

That One Wonderful, Terrible, Unforgettable Halloween

By Judith Rogers

The Depression was pretty much over in the late '30s, but prosperity hadn't yet found its way to our small Ohio farm. My father worked hard to make ends meet, however skimpily, in those days. If he wasn't working the fields with our two sturdy Morgan horses, Kate and Liz, he'd be milking our eight cows, tending to the hogs or feeding the chickens which laid the eggs he sold in Barberton for a scant 10 cents a dozen.

I was the baby of the family (how I hated to hear myself called that!), the fourth child and only girl. Mama is fond of recalling how she cried when she learned I was on the way. After three strapping boys, all she could envision was another pair of overalls on that already-sagging clothesline. I guess she was sorry clear up to the minute I was born there in our farmhouse. But when the doctor slapped me, looked at Mama and beamingly exclaimed, "It's a girl!" the sorrow disappeared and all she could do was murmur over and over, "Isn't she sweet! Isn't she sweet!" "I couldn't even see you because my eyes were closed," she would tell me in later years, "but I knew you couldn't be anything but sweet.

Many hilarious and other not-so-hilarious incidents float to the surface of my mind in recalling those years on the farm, but an event which looms large in my memory is that one particular Halloween night in 1939.

Living on a farm before these noisy days of television meant that we had to create our own fun, and create we did.

We were too far from other farms for neighborhood parties, so we had our own special Halloween ritual. Early in the day we four scoured the pumpkin patch for exactly the right ones we needed. Then, armed with pencils for marking lines, knives for cutting and lots of old paper for the mess we were making, we turned out some pretty fair pumpkin faces. Being only 4, I, of course, had help with mine, but I can still remember that particular scary face.

The day seemed terribly long since nothing much happens on Halloween before dark.

Bob, as the eldest, had the privilege of lighting the silent waiting faces. One by one, the terrible scowling jack-o'-lanterns came alive, and we stood entranced.

I slowly turned around, hoping to see nothing more than a dark empty yard; but there, creeping stealthily around the side of the house and heading straight for us, was a huge black thing—arms outstretched—with just a big black lump for a face and covered with a limp old hat.

I wanted to scream! I wanted to run. My usually active mouth was frozen shut. Bob, Theo and David were mumbling incantations and staring at the jack-o'-lanterns while all I could do was stand, transfixed.

"Aargh," growled the thing as it came closer and started to grab for Theo, who took off like a bolt of lightning when he quickly glanced around. Bob and David started yelling and running with that thing first chasing one, then the other, then the other.

I regained control of my legs and tore to the safety of the house. There on the porch I stood, beside an unusually calm mother—Mama, who screams at the slightest provocation.

"Are you Wally Beichler?" she cried.

"No-o-o," came back a slow reply.

The boys disappeared, hollering all the way down to the peep house with that thing steadily plodding on behind them. It was now threatening in a low, slow monotone as it ran, "I'm gonna git you, I'm gonna git you."

With this, the boys would spread out and the thing would again chase one, then the other, while they tried desperately to lose their pursuer.

"Mama, where's Daddy?" I suddenly asked.

"Oh, he's probably in the front room reading or listening to the radio."

Strange that he hadn't heard all the commotion, I thought, and ran in to tell him what was going on. He wasn't there. He wasn't anywhere I looked!

Back to the porch I ran, where the chase was still going on.

"Are you Ben Steiner?" Mama persisted as the thing came thudding by again.

"No-o-o," it panted.

"Mama, is that Daddy out there?" I asked, revelation finally beginning to dawn.

"Why? Isn't he in the front room?"

"No, I looked everywhere. That is Daddy, isn't it?"

"Well," she smiled, "it just might be."

The chase was noticeably slowing down as three frightened boys and one tired, warmly overdressed father were quickly wearing out. Finally they all dropped to the ground by the porch step when It called to my mother, "Frieda, come out here and help me out of this durned outfit." Then, huffing and puffing as a 225-pound man with some unexpected excessive exercise would, he looked at the boys and laughed.

"Well, I had you all fooled, didn't I?"

"No, you didn't," Bob retorted. "I knew you all the time!"

"Why did you run so hard then?" roared Daddy.

"I knew it was you when you almost got me at the chicken house," Theo remembered. "I recognized your voice!"

"I knew it was you all the time, too," fibbed David.

"I knew it was you, too, Daddy," I piped in—still from the safety of the porch. "You weren't in your chair."

And then we laughed—oh, how we laughed. Pumpkin faces and Halloween rituals forgotten, we all lived and relived that chase over cookies and cider till bedtime. Who had more fun? A hardworking father who still had enough energy and imagination to turn an average Halloween into a memorable one, or we four, still slightly weak children, who claim to this day that we knew it was him all the time?

Psychologists today would no doubt blame all sorts of frustrations on parents creating a frantic madcap chase scene as that one was. I only know that my three well-adjusted brothers and I fondly recall that horror-filled night 30-odd years ago with belly-aching laughter, and we all agree that it was, indeed, one unforgettable Halloween! ❖

Pranks on the Path

By Marsha Kay Wilder

My grandfather had a very exciting and mischievous life as a boy. Today, his memories are a novelty for both young and old to hear. This is the story I like and remember best.

It was Halloween and, as in the city today, boys and girls in the country celebrated this season with tricks and treats. Too often we awake the day after to find overturned trash cans and soaped windows. When Grandpa was a boy, there were few trash cans on the farm. Leftover food was fed to the pigs and papers were burned. There were, however, numerous objects to overturn. Every farm had one and the challenge was great. There was also an amount of danger involved for, as you know, an outhouse is far heavier than a mere trash can.

This particular Halloween Grandfather and a friend of his had decided to overturn their neighbors' outside toilets. One especially unique family lived just down the road— Mrs. Jones, a stout woman of 300 or so pounds, and her husband, Terrance, who weighed no more than 100 pounds fully dressed. The little man had watchful eyes and a quick temper.

The night came. It was dark and quiet. Grandpa and Pal sneaked to both sides of the outhouse. One, two, heave!

The outhouse would not budge. Grandpa would not let it get the best of him! He moved to the nearby woodpile and grabbed a piece of wood. His friend followed suit, and before long they had lifted the outhouse about a foot off the ground.

The moon had come out from behind the clouds and was reflecting off two white posts beneath the structure the boys were moving. The fact that these posts were attached to the gargantuan Mrs. Jones was soon to be discovered. Her wails for help startled the boys so that when they regained their senses, it was nearly too late. Mr. Jones had already arrived on the scene with shotgun in hand. Grandfather ran.

Sometime later, Grandfather saw Pal. He had not seen him since that night. He asked Pal how it was that he had escaped so quickly.

It seemed that while Pal was running away as fast as Grandfather was, there had been a clothesline strung in Pal's path which caught him in the neck and threw him backward into the tall grass. There he lay for what seemed like hours, hardly breathing, for fear that Mr. Jones and his shotgun were close by.

Needless to say, Grandfather and Pal avoided the Jones place the following Halloween. ✤

A Thanksgiving Memory

By Fred Droddy

In our book of memories, we probably recall some holiday adventure that is dearer to us than all the rest. There is one that is very special to me, special because it was the only time I can remember seeing my paternal grandfather. I never knew my grandmother, as she passed away some years before that Thanksgiving Day.

My mother would never mention holiday plans to us children until she was sure of them. She knew how easily children can be disappointed if things don't turn out as planned.

It was still dark when we children were aroused in the early morning hours and had breakfast by the light of a kerosene lamp. After eating, my father went to hitch the horses to the old spring wagon. Mother dressed us in our warmest clothes. It wasn't very long until everyone was ready to travel.

The air was crisp and cold as we started out, and had the feel of more snow. The steel tires on the wheels made a complaining screech as they pressed through the 4 or 5 inches of snow already on the ground. The road wound its way through the pines still laden with last night's snow and we could see tracks of wild animals, mostly deer, where they crossed and recrossed the road.

That part of the country was sparsely settled in those days; we did pass near a log cabin or two set back from the road in the pines.

It was rough going for the horses, and we had to stop several times to let them rest. The steam from their sweating hides rose in the cold air and frost had formed around their nostrils.

Later in the day we stopped. Dad built a fire beside the road and fed the horses a small amount of hay and also some grain from a nose bag. We had cold sandwiches for our lunch. After reheating the foot stones, we were on our way again.

It started snowing very slowly shortly after we had lunched. The falling flakes seemed to caress our faces ever so softly when we looked upward. By midafternoon, it quit snowing and became much colder.

As time passed by, the novelty of the trip was wearing off and we children were becoming impatient, as most children do after a time. It

> *My mother would never mention holiday plans to us children because she knew how easily children can be disappointed if things don't turn out as planned.*

was starting to get dark and the cold was creeping in on us. The stones were no longer keeping us warm and Dad kept reminding us it was only a little further.

Eventually we emerged from the timber and, across the field, we could see the glimmer of a light; then I warmed in anticipation of seeing my grandfather. The old potbellied stove in the parlor was a welcome sight with its glowing fire.

Next morning, I went to the barn with Grandpa to watch him milk the cow and feed the chickens and other animals. That was when I learned that milk came from cows, not cans, as I had always thought. I also learned that day where eggs came from—and refused to eat eggs for some time.

After supper that evening, I recall listening to Grandpa tell of the hard times he and Grandma had while homesteading this 160-acre ranch. Three girls and one boy were born and raised here. My dad was next to the youngest.

I also remember Grandpa telling Dad that a cougar had been reported in the area. Grandpa said he had seen some tracks back in the timber away from the ranch. (Later this cougar was killed by my Grandpa and was the last one ever heard of in that territory.)

The days we spent on the ranch were exciting days for me. There were dogs, cats, cows, pigs, horses. It seemed Grandpa had them all. He even had a pet deer that occasionally came around the ranch. It would not let us touch it, but Grandpa could pet it. He had found the deer early the previous summer when it was a very young fawn. Evidently something had happened to its mother. The poor thing was weak from hunger. Grandpa carried it home and fed it from an improvised bottle until it was strong enough to be on its own. Then he turned it loose and it hung around the ranch. Sometimes it would be gone for several days, but it always came back to the ranch.

Thanksgiving Day arrived clear and cold. The sun was shining brightly, but it didn't warm the air very much. Mother started cooking the dinner as soon as breakfast was over. I remember Dad going to a lean-to shed at the back of the house to get a venison roast. (We had no turkey.) It was frozen so hard Dad had to take it to the woodpile and cut it with an ax. The venison was one Grandpa had got prior to our arrival.

We ate dinner sometime after noon. For the meal we had roast venison with dressing, mashed potatoes, gravy, hot homemade bread with fresh ranch butter and wild raspberry jam, wild gooseberry pie, cold milk or buttermilk, whichever we chose. I can still recall the aroma of the dinner cooking and how good it tasted.

After dinner, Grandpa wanted to show off his matched pair of pinto ponies and the things he had taught them to do. They were a beautiful team, white with tan blotches. It had taken much time and patience to train them, but Grandpa said time was something he had lots of.

We went out to the corral and he put them through their paces, making them do the many tricks he had taught them to do. They were trained to do these tricks to the crack of a small whip and Grandpa's low, commanding voice. After each trick, he would give the ponies a little sugar from his hand. The pet deer came from the timber and I ran to the house to get some bread for her. She nibbled at the bread from our hands and we really thought this was something.

Later, when the chores were done and we had eaten some of the leftovers from dinner, we sat around the fire in the parlor. Grandpa took his banjo down from the wall, Dad played the mouth organ and Mother sang, with us children joining in occasionally. Mother had a beautiful voice and used to sing often to us children.

The 10 days we spent there were over too soon, and we left early one morning for the long trip home. It was snowing lightly the morning we left, and I remember Grandpa standing by the house and waving to us as we entered the timber across the field.

Shortly after that, Grandpa sold the old place and moved to Idaho, where he later passed away. That was the only time I ever saw him, but his memory will be cherished throughout my life. ❖

The Saga of Sally

By Christine O'Brien

My grandmother laid aside her sewing, went to the door, and glancing at the sky, she said, "Come on kids. We better go get the chickens inside. It looks like it is going to rain."

We discovered that one old hen had not taken her chicks to the shelter as she was supposed to. This time she had squatted down under a bush and all the little chickens under her seemed to be dead. Grandmother gathered them into her apron and took them inside. One little yellow chick was still alive. Since only one had survived, grandmother said I could have it for a pet. I named it Sally.

It became apparent that Sally was the wrong name, because he was fast growing into a fine young rooster. He was a great pet at first, but as he became more and more attached to me he developed a violent dislike for any other woman or girl. Men or boys he ignored.

Not having modern plumbing, whenever my grandmother took the little path out to the back, I either had to go out and keep Sally occupied or Grandmother had to carry a stick to ward Sally off.

Shortly before Thanksgiving, Sally chased a neighbor lady out of yard and spurred Grandmother when she went to the rescue. My Grandmother said, "That does it. Sally is going to make a good roast for Thanksgiving."

Needless to say I was very upset. From then on, each night when I said my prayers I asked God to save Sally's life some way.

The day before Thankgiving a neighbor brought over a turkey already dressed and ready to cook. They had bought a turkey and then the man had won a turkey at a store contest. Since they couldn't use two, they brought one to us, and Sally was safe for the time being.

However, Sally's manners did not improve, so my grandmother said she would surely cook him for Christmas dinner.

One day about three days before Christmas, a man came to deliver a load of wood to us. Sally came running up to me and Mr. Matlock said to Grandad, "That sure is a fine rooster. How about selling him to me? I have a lot of hens but no rooster."

Grandad said, "The rooster belongs to Christine. You will have to ask her."

At first I didn't know what to say. After waiting a few minutes Mr. Matlock said, "I'll give you 50 cents for him."

I turned to Grandad and asked him if 50 cents would buy meat for our dinner, because I knew if I sold Sally and we weren't able to buy meat for Christmas dinner, I would be in trouble with Grandmother. Grandad said he was sure that 50 cents would buy the meat.

I told Mr. Matlock that he could buy Sally. Mr. Matlock took Sally and gave me the money. I took it inside and gave it to my grandmother; I think she was relieved not to have to kill Sally.

A month or two later I saw Mr. Matlock. I asked him about Sally. He said Sally was fat and sassy, but Mr. Matlock said he always had to feed the chickens and gather the eggs. Sally would not let Mrs. Matlock in the chicken pen. ❖

Winter Days

A few years back, we had one of those heavy, wet snows for which February can be famous. Janice and I have always loved the snow, so it didn't really bother us too much when there was a couple of feet of the white stuff in the front yard of the old home place.

It sure did bother a lot of younger folks, though. We were amazed as people got downright panicky from not being able to get out and about for a couple of days during the worst of the storm. Electricity and telephone services were out for a day or so (wet snow, tree branches and power lines don't mix), and that added to the general feeling of privation for a lot of folks.

Janice and I just burrowed in and enjoyed it. We were prepared for such "crises" by life when things were not so taken for granted.

The old kerosene lamp stood at the ready for lighting, just awaiting a good trimming. We grew up knowing what life without electricity was, so it wasn't a shock to our systems. Even after rural electrification was delivered to Mama and Daddy's farm, for a long time outages were only a small thunderstorm away. We always kept our lamp ready for such times. The only difference today is that Janice *did* convince me to substitute a more delicate-smelling fuel instead of coal oil or kerosene.

Telephones? We didn't have them when we were growing up. My parents didn't get one until all of us kids were grown and gone; Janice's folks never did have one. So the absence of that bothersome ringing device was something I neither needed nor missed.

We still have a wood-burning stove in the house and, though my back complains a little more each year, I stack in a pretty good amount of seasoned wood and kindling on the porch when the weatherman is predicting a substantial storm. Janice loves to fix hot chocolate or apple cider and cinnamon on a cold night and listen to the popping of the oak and hickory in that trusty old heater. No snow robs us of power for warming our old farmhouse.

Our my "stock up and stack in" mentality is still with us from years when we didn't make it into town for shopping very often, so that means the pantry is usually filled with supplies.

All in all, I was happy we got that heavy snow. It reminded me of the blessings we have in this great country, and how we so often take them for granted. It also reminded me of the lessons of self-sufficiency Janice and I learned on the farm in the days of our youth. I know you'll enjoy these farm stories of winter days back in the Good Old Days.

—*Ken Tate*

John Slobodnik

The Iron Pump

By Vivian Branson

During my seventh summer, Mr. Ferguson, our neighbor to the north, drilled a water well. For a week, Duane and I spent every waking moment watching the machine make the bore.

The huge derrick towered over us. At last the casing was slipped into place. The pump was lifted high in the air and carefully lowered into the opening.

It was a handsome iron pump with a handle that went up and down. How I envied Mr. Ferguson's children.

Our own water supply came from a well on the back porch, but we had to draw the water with a rope and bucket. The bucket was a long slender tube lowered into the well by a rope threaded through a pulley and suspended from the roof. A wooden plug floated free in the bottom of the tube so it could fill from the lower end.

The plug fell in place, filling the tube's end, while the water was brought up hand over hand with the rope. When the filled tube was pushed into a bucket, the plug was released and the water came gushing out. A knot in the rope held the tube just below the top of the casing when it was not in use.

The filled granite bucket and a washbasin had a permanent place on the washstand near the back door. Above them hung a towel and a gray enameled dipper.

How I longed for an iron pump like the beauty that stood in the Fergusons' yard.

Before we were allowed to pump, a connecting pipe was cupped over the end of the spout. It led to a stock tank in the barnyard. We took turns at the pump handle, watching as the fresh, clear water gushed into the cup and disappeared into the pipe. The area around the pump became a muddy mess, but I was the one who continued pumping up and down, up and down. At last Mr. Ferguson protested that the stock tank was overflowing and the barnyard was knee-deep in mud.

My love affair with that iron pump continued through fall and on into the gusty cold winter. The ridicule of my family and friends only made me more stubborn and loyal to it. I pumped at every opportunity. I was unyielding in my dedication to that pump.

My disillusionment came with destructive and agonizing suddenness on the coldest day of winter.

Charles Ferguson dared me to lick the pump handle. I was puzzled by the dare, but to my 7-year-old mind it seemed a reasonable thing to do.

I did it! I put my tongue against that frosty pump handle!

I shed my infatuation and the outer layer of my tongue in the same painful instant. ❖

> *It was a handsome iron pump with a handle that went up and down. How I envied Mr. Ferguson's children.*

The Christmas Pageant

By Opal Waymire Beaty

In the early 1920s, before the days of radio in our area of Oklahoma, the only weather forecast we had was that pronounced by Dad when he entered the house after milking the cows early each morning.

"Sure looks like a blizzard today. Better not try to go to school. None of the kids will come out in a storm like this, not if they're bright!"

But I was the teacher—I had to go. I had a strong feeling that the "kids" would come also, in spite of the storm, because this was the day for the Christmas pageant.

There was no use trying to start the Model-T and I couldn't subject my riding horse, Nellie, to the ordeal of standing unprotected in a storm all day. I walked the mile and a half to school, weighed down with my tin lunch pail and properties for the pageant. Flakes of snow mixed with pellets of ice stung my face, and each breath of the icy air seemed to cut my lungs like a knife. My feet were so numb that I almost fell into the room when I opened the schoolhouse door.

Little Beaver School was a one-room rural school in northern Oklahoma, located on Little Beaver Creek. Teaching in a rural school in those days was cozy and intimate. The enrollment of 21 pupils from the first grade through the eighth represented 10 families, all living within a 2-mile radius of the school, and they all walked. Although there was a course of study to be followed, and the county superintendent visited once or twice a year for an hour or so, the teacher was on his or her own and considerable flexibility was possible.

I laid the crumpled paper, wood shavings and lumps of coal in the big black heater; the lighted matches kept dropping from my stiff fingers, but on the third try, the paper ignited and tiny yellow tongues of flame coaxed the fine pine shavings into larger flames which, in turn, folded around the glistening lumps of black coal, heating them to the point of combustion. The fire was started!

I became warm and drowsy and was tempted to sit by the stove, but there was much to do before our guests arrived in the afternoon.

I surveyed the room. In each window were Christmas trees cut out

Continued on page 138

of green construction paper, looking like cookies with green icing. On the front blackboard were three drawings: a calendar of the month, a jolly Santa, and a group of angels and shepherds. These had been made by holding commercial stencils of thin paper with many tiny perforations on the board and patting over them, very gently, with chalk-filled blackboard erasers.

It was a special favor to the younger children to rub chalk heavily on the chalkboard and erase it, repeatedly, until the erasers oozed chalk dust. The taller pupils applied the stencils and filled in the outlines with colored chalks. There were no school funds for such extras, so the teacher purchased the stencils and colored chalk out of her $90-a-month salary.

The snow was falling faster and thicker, the wind was rising, and I questioned myself, *Will the pupils show up?* Then I heard the sounds of stomping feet and young voices calling "Merry Christmas!"

I was not surprised. Neither was I surprised at the white spots on red cheeks and noses which indicated frostbite. The children lumbered into the room so heavily wrapped that I wondered whether they had walked or rolled from their homes. They, too, were carrying lunch pails and bulging packages of items for the afternoon program.

The packages were piled on my desk and the lunch pails were stored in the heated classroom instead of the unheated cloakroom. Older boys gathered snow in the one washbasin and the metal wastebasket from which we treated frosted feet, fingers and cheeks. It wasn't until years later that I learned that we had used the wrong method of first-aid.

As soon as they thawed, the pupils were

eager to get the room in order for the parents and younger brothers and sisters who would arrive soon after lunch for the program. Books and tablets, pens and pencils were neatly stacked inside the desks; bottles of ink were gathered and stored on a top shelf of the bookcase; the side blackboards were washed and chalk trays and erasers were cleaned.

The most excitement centered around the decorating of the Christmas tree. In the Little Beaver community, it was not customary to have Christmas trees in the homes, so this was a special treat. No evergreens grew in the area, so the older boys had cut a well-shaped bough from a tree on the bank of Little Beaver Creek and stood it in a bucket of soil. It was barren and quite "unbeautiful," which didn't bother us a bit for it was what we were accustomed to. Everyone in the school had a part in converting it into a truly beautiful tree.

The Christmas tree was barren and quite "unbeautiful," which didn't bother us a bit for it was what we were accustomed to.

The taller girls carefully covered each branch and twig with cotton. A group of little girls, with needles and long double strands of cotton thread, sat in one corner stringing cranberries; younger boys, in another corner, tried to string popcorn, but ate more than they strung. Small wax candles of many colors were placed in tin holders and clipped to the branches.

When the decorating was completed, the tree resembled a matron dressed in ermine, adorned with rubies and pearls. I shudder now when I remember that I was so thoughtless as to take such chances with lighted candles on a cotton-trimmed tree in a room filled with people. However, several pupils were assigned to watch for fire.

The final rehearsal of the pageant did not go so well. We were tired and hungry; also, this was the first time the actors had seen each other in costume, which caused a lot of giggling. One of the Wise Men had a little hassle with a shepherd; Joseph suddenly became self-conscious about going down the aisle with Mary, a girl he had known all of his life; an angel quarreled with the innkeeper over a piece of candy.

After the rehearsal, we settled down to a dreary lunch period. A nauseating wave of smells drifted through the room: dill pickles, apples and fried meat mingled with the odors of drying wool and leather.

The snow stopped and the wind died after lunch, and the school yard began filling with horse-drawn wagons. Women and children emerged from cocoons of blankets and quilts; men, wearing mackinaws, caps with fur-lined earflaps and fur-lined boots, brushed at frozen mustaches with heavily mittened hands.

When all were unwrapped and warmed, the pageant began. The little angels sang softly *a cappella Joy to the World, Hark, the Herald Angels Sing* and *O Little Town of Bethlehem.* A girl dressed in a soft red wool dress, hair tightly braided in pigtails, told in a clear voice the story of the Nativity as the characters proceeded from the cloakroom down the center aisle to the front of the room.

The stage was the small, well-worn space between the teacher's desk and the heater; the only footlights were the lights of wonder in the eyes of the small children sitting on their mothers' laps and the glow of pride in the eyes of the parents. The backdrop was the white Christmas tree with its lighted candles flickering uncertainly as though afraid the children might bobble.

An angel stepped forth from the singing group and made a prediction. Joseph and Mary, turned away by an unsympathetic innkeeper, went to a stable; shepherds were awed and "sore afraid"; Wise Men from the East felt less wise upon seeing a star in the heavens which they had never noticed before; and so the beautiful story unfolded.

The children were impressed, the parents nodded approvingly, but the teacher saw it with double vision. After a strenuous day, an inadequate cold lunch, with frosty feet and a bursting head, I was not quite convinced of the authenticity of the characters.

As they proceeded out of the cloakroom again at a grand finale and joined in the final chorus, I began to see with clarity. Joseph was only a young boy in a huge army coat which dragged at his heels, and Mary was a little neighbor girl carrying her favorite doll. The angels were children who only a couple of hours ago were reaching into tin buckets with grimy hands for cold biscuit-and-fried-meat sandwiches. The three Wise Men were not persons at all, but Dad's maroon-and-gray horse blanket, Mom's blue-and-white bedspread and an old Indian rug from the top of my cedar chest at home.

The idea of these three inanimate household objects walking down the aisle struck me as being funny. I glanced across the room at Dad, and he must have been thinking the same thing. He winked, and placed his big hand over his mouth as though to stroke his mustache, but I knew it was to cover a wide grin. For one terrible moment I struggled between tears and laughter, and turned back to the cloakroom to blow my nose and wipe my eyes.

The transition from the world of imagination to that of reality is not difficult for children. After the pageant came the treats for everyone in the school community. Hard Christmas candies purchased by the wooden bucketful and oranges purchased by the crate had been stuffed into stockings made of red tarlatan by Mom and me. The treats were gifts from the teacher and were no small item in her limited budge.

As I rode home that afternoon in the wagon with Dad, I reviewed the day's events. The struggle with the storm, the hours of hard physical work, and the strain of not knowing what to expect from either the children or the weather, was followed by the warm glow of knowing that the Christmas pageant had come off quite well. The joy of the pupils and the appreciation of the parents was evident, although not expressed in words. *This*, I reflected, *is part of what teaching is all about.*

Although Christmas with my family still was several days off, as far as I was concerned, it terminated with the Christmas pageant at Little Beaver School. ❖

The Party Line

By Barbara Wilcox Scafferi

When I think of the party line, I'm not thinking of what the Republicans or Democrats are currently proposing. I am remembering the old country telephone lines when we had eight parties on the line.

We are so used to the privacy of private lines these days that the idea of seven other people monitoring our conversations seems unbelievable.

What if you were a real chatty person, one who likes to get on the phone and talk for 20 minutes to an hour? Seven other people may want to use the line. No problem. After what seemed a reasonable time one simply said, "Helen, I need to use the phone."

Usually, the person talking would say, "Okay, I'll be done in a minute"—and so it went.

There was a lady on *our* line named Letty. Letty spent most of her day either talking on the phone or listening in on other people's conversations. We all knew she did this. I remember one time when Mother really wanted some privacy and, being pretty sure that Letty was listening said, "Letty, get off the line."

Letty was honest. She replied "Okay," and hung up.

One year, the day before Easter, our brooder house caught on fire. As usual, the party line was in use. Mother said, "Mabel, I have to use the phone to call the fire department." Mabel immediately relinquished the line. Before the fire department arrived, many of the neighbors had come, as word spread on the party line.

Years later, when my husband and I lived in the old brick farmhouse we rented from my parents, the party line was down to four instead of eight. One fall day, sparks from the trash burner had ignited some dry grass. I ran to the phone to call my parents. The line was in use. "Vivian, I need to call my folks as I have little fires in our yard." She gave up the phone immediately. Before Mother arrived, Vivian had already gotten there.

The days of the party line are pretty much part of the good old days now. We have more privacy for our conversations, but we don't have neighbors coming to immediate assistance in times of trouble as when the word was spread by the party line. ❖

The days of the party line are part of the good old days now. We have more privacy for our conversations, but we don't have neighbors coming to immediate assistance in times of trouble.

Our Christmas Spirit

By Edwin Christenson

*I*n the early 1900s before radios, dreaming of a white Christmas, or *Rudolph the Red-Nosed Reindeer,* we were nevertheless well aware of the Christmas season.

Dad, Mother, my two brothers and a sister were living in a two-story log house on a farm near Ellsworth, Wis. This was in horse-and-buggy days, although horseless carriages had been seen in town.

We attended school in the white one-room schoolhouse, and we were lucky to have only a half-mile to travel. Our teacher, who taught all eight grades and 35 pupils, brought colored paper for us to cut into strips and paste together in chains for tree decorations at our homes.

Shopping for presents in Ellsworth five miles away meant riding in a sleigh pulled by a not-so-fast team of workhorses. There were some good selections in the stores for our nickels and dimes in those years, but of course children then didn't expect so much, either.

Dad made skis and sleds for us, and one day near Christmas he wasn't watching the clock very closely and as we came home from school, he almost got caught with two pairs of skis being steamed "to be bent" in the wash boiler on the kitchen range.

As the time drew near for Christmas Eve, the days were much too short for Mother. Willing hands carried water and wood to the kitchen, even though the reservoir on the range held several pails of water and the wood box had room for armloads of wood. We did those chores all winter, but not with as much enthusiasm as we did near Christmas.

How different were those years of getting ready for Christmas. Mother was busy late into the evenings baking varieties of cookies—*sandbakkelse, krumkake* and so forth. Then there were varieties of meat to prepare—headcheese, rolls, *polse* and wonderful home-prepared pork sausage. Ale was made from roasted barley, sugar, hops and yeast and left to brew in a big stone crock. It was not strong but had a very pleasant flavor. But alas, now, no one we know can remember the recipe—and there are no more big stone crocks.

The day of Christmas Eve Mother saw the big clock on the mantel going altogether too fast. Time was running away from her. The house had to be sparkling clean. The oak floors were scrubbed almost white

The day of Christmas Eve Mother saw the big clock on the mantel going altogether too fast.

with strong homemade soap. The stoves were polished and the windows washed. It's hard to believe nowadays, but then there was not one Christmas decoration up yet. The tree, too, was still outside.

Two bachelor uncles, Jake and John, lived on a farm down the road a little way from us, and they were invited to be with us for the Christmas Eve dinner. We were always excited about their coming, as they had interesting packages with them.

We pressed our noses against the freshly washed windows to see when the lights went out in the uncles' house; then we knew they were on their way to be with us. I'm sure it was a treat for them to have a fine dinner and they enjoyed our excitement and the Christmas spirit.

Finally the food was on the table, and everything was delicious, but we always thought Dad, Mother and the uncles talked too much; it took so long before they were ready to leave the table. We were waiting for them so we could help clear the table and get the dishes washed.

Not until then would there be any decorations up, but we children had to run upstairs and stay there until everything was ready, which meant the tree was set up and the paper chains and popcorn strings arranged on it. Also the beautiful candles in the candle holders were lit. The presents were brought out from their hiding places and placed under the tree.

We wondered why it should take so long, but just imagine how much there was to do! Arranging the candles and lighting them took some time. The uncles helped with the tree and I'm sure they were happy to have a part in it,

but we were getting impatient and called down, "Aren't you ready yet?"

"Be quiet, we'll soon be ready," came the answer.

"Now you can come," Mother called, and I can tell you we wasted no time coming down the steep stairway.

What a wonderful sight greeted us! There was that big spruce tree all glowing and sparkling with those beautiful candles. Even the presents were not noticed for a few minutes.

We were not to have our presents yet. We had learned some things to recite, but we went through that too fast, Mother said. Dad read the Christmas story and Mother, who had a good voice, led us in singing Christmas hymns.

Ah, at last the presents were distributed, and then it was as it is nowadays, as one of our grandsons said of opening presents last Christmas, "It's utter confusion."

Our uncles helped us play with our new toys, and they were with us until late in the evening when we had *fattigman* rosettes and that good ale.

Christmas Day meant getting up early, doing the farm chores and going to church in the big sled with robes over us and, if it was very cold, hot bricks for our feet. But regardless of weather we always got to church.

It was a tradition with our families to go visiting up to two weeks after Christmas. We had many uncles and aunts and, of course, many cousins. They all usually got together at each others' homes and the cousins really enjoyed the Christmas visiting. Life was much simpler those years, but the Christmas spirit was very strong in us.❖

John Slobodnik

Lighting the Way

By Helen Marie Barnhart

The sky was darkening on that afternoon in the year of 1916. My older sister Dora and brother Sam were holding tightly to my hands as we hurried home from school. The teacher made it very clear that we were not to loiter or play on our way home. We were to go straight home, as a snowstorm was coming in.

We lived about a mile from the schoolhouse near the little town of Tuttle on a small dairy farm that supplied the townsfolk with all the dairy products.

Every child was taught very early in life the danger of being caught out in a snowstorm. You can lose all sense of direction when the snow gets so dense you can't see your hand before your face. There were many cases in our territory where people were found frozen to death after the spring thaws.

I was only 6, and this was my first experience with a real live blizzard. Even though it was only 3 o'clock in the afternoon, it was almost dark by the time we reached our front porch. The first flakes were coming down.

Mother was baking bread at the big old-fashioned cookstove. My! How good it smelled as she pulled those golden brown loaves from the oven. Our usual snack when we came home from school was a large slice of bread with rich, thick sour cream spread on it with just a sprinkling of sugar.

On this particular afternoon, Mother told us she would have to go to the barn and tend the animals. Our father would not be home, as he was spending the night at Bismarck on business.

Mama put on her snowshoes and a heavy mackintosh; then, wrapping a long, woolen scarf around her head and neck, she started off for the barn before the storm began to worsen. We had not put up the rope we held onto as we went from the house to the barn. You could feel along this rope and not lose your way, even in the worst kind of storm.

Children have no sense of time; they go by their feelings. We didn't know what time it was, but we knew something was wrong when the windows became dark; the rooms were becoming cold because the fires were dying down. The younger children, as well as the 3-month-old baby, were crying for something to eat. There was a large potbellied stove in the living room and a small stove in each of the bedrooms, as well as the stove in the kitchen. The thing that made it worse was all of us children, until we reached the age of 12, were not allowed to handle the stoves, or fires.

Dora, who was the oldest of us children but only 10 herself, had never before been put in a position where she had to take all the responsibility. She threw open the door, but all we could see was cold, blinding snow so thick you couldn't see a foot in front of you.

Closing the door, she stood there with her back to the door, with the most ashen face. We could feel her fear as well as see it. It was all around us—the cooling stoves and the crying children, as well as the howling wind.

Then Dora seemed to change before our eyes; she changed from a fearful child into a determined, forceful woman.

"Sam, bring me all the lamps, candles and matches you can find," she said.

Pushing the table under the window that was facing the barn, she started lighting all the lamps and candles as Sam brought them to her.

"Now bring me all the mirrors in the house, Sam," she said. Then, placing chairs near the back of the table, she braced the mirrors on them so that the lamps would reflect their light more brilliantly onto the window.

Then Sam said, "Remember how we always ran outside to watch the sparks and burning bits of paper when Mama cleaned the chimneys?"

"Yes," we answered.

This gave us another idea. It took us only a few minutes to gather all the paper, magazines and cardboard we could find. Dora crammed the papers in as fast as we brought them to her.

Soon the stovepipes were red, as the lighted papers went flying over the house. When the papers were all burned up, we looked at each other for a new suggestion we might try to help our dear mother out there in the storm.

It was then we heard a new sound; it was as though something had fallen against the door. When Dora opened the door, there was Mama, lying on the front porch more dead than alive. All of us older children got a hold on her clothing and dragged her into the house, closing the door. Sam ran for some blankets to roll her in, while Dora stoked the stoves to get the house nice and warm. We took turns rubbing her hands and feet. When she finally opened her eyes, she saw five frightened children looking down at her. The baby had cried itself to sleep.

It was several days before Mama could tell us what had happened to her after she had left us to go to the barn. This is what she related:

"When I got to the barn, I milked all the cows, even though it was early, fearing I couldn't make it back later. By this time I had lit the lantern, but when I opened the door to go back to the house, I knew the lantern would do me no good. I couldn't see my hand in front of my face. The thought did come to me, I could stay in the barn and crawl into the hay to keep warm until the storm was over. I knew I had to get back to you children; the baby would have to be nursed. The fires would need tending.

"Walking through high drifts of snow soon taxed my strength, as I also realized I had missed the house and lost my sense of direction. I thought, *They will find my body in the spring when the snow is melted.* I kept walking and finally came up against the fence for the pasture, but what part of that vast fencing was I holding to? Standing there, afraid to start walking in either direction, I began to pray.

"God becomes real and very comforting in a time of great peril. While I was praying, I thought I saw a star. I knew this could not be, for the thickness of the clouds and snow would not allow a star to show through. There it was again, and right below it was a glow that I could not explain.

"Turning loose of the fence, I went in a straight line for that faint glow. It was sheer willpower that kept me going on. When I ran into the side of the house, I felt myself along the wall till I reached the porch."

When Papa got home, you can be sure the rope went up. Never again did we take a chance of being unprepared for those killer storms.

Mama said it taught her one thing—"that children can be depended on." ❖

Endearing Memories

By Pat Murphy

If I were to be picked up and transported blindfolded back through time and set down in Aunt Ethel and Uncle Lon's farmhouse at dawn on a wintry morning, I would know immediately where I was. I would again hear the chunking sound of an ax splitting kindling wood to be burned in the kitchen stove and the heating stove standing on smooth, silvery curved legs in the living room. I would revel in the sound of milk pails clanging together, and the squeak and rasp of the pump handle. The crowing of the rooster, without which day would hardly dare to begin, and the mourning doves cooing softly to each other in the mammoth pine trees.

And the smells, oh the smells that will endure ever in my mind! The old farmhouse had an aura about it. The pungent aroma of smoke from a wood fire mingled with that of fresh, strong coffee brewing beside crackling bacon and simmering eggs. The tantalizing, heady smell of yeast bread already rising on the back of the stove. Even the faint odor of slightly damp dog fur from Major, the shepherd, who lay close by the potbellied stove all night.

Outside, my nose would be greeted by the rich, grainy smell of mash as it was scattered to the pecking, scurrying chickens diving about willy-nilly among the guinea hens and ducks. Farther on, my nose welcomed the earthy smell of hay from the barn interlaced with that of the warm, genial cows and horses. Each is a part of my memories.

Then, blindfold off at last, I would love again the sight of the worn amber logs that hug the outside of the snug, rambling farmhouse; the multicolored rag rugs inside the back door; starched fresh curtains framing windows; and the kitchen table inevitably covered with shining oilcloth.

If the morning sunlight had not yet stretched over the hill and tumbled through the windows, perhaps the kerosene lamp with its gleaming glass chimney would be glowing in the center of the table, casting soft feelers of light into the far corners of the room. The brass hooks behind the door would still be there to hold hats and coats, and the worn-smooth wooden stool would be there beside them, waiting for someone to sit and wrestle off heavy wet boots.

In the living room I know I would find the overstuffed furniture with its faded floral covering; the huge, highly polished radio with its many dials; and the wooden-runged chairs around the potbellied monster where we could set, lean back and prop our chilled feet up on the rail…. All would be the same.

I know that upstairs, in air so frosty in the morning that noses tingled, will be the deep, plump feather beds, with bright, patchwork, thick-as-your-arm comforters over them. Candles in wax-dripped holders, used to light the way up to bed, would sit on the old metal trunks that doubled as storage and nightstands.

Over the bare wooden floors, the many bright rag rugs that helped cold feet find their way down to the warm kitchen would lie flat and clean in the same short-hop-apart spaces from bedside to the top of the stairs.

Most of all, there would be Aunt Ethel, eyes as bright as stars, to say, "Come, set a spell." Uncle Lon, weatherworn and rugged, would add in his customary slow drawl, "Come on in from the cold, here by the fire, and warm your feet." ❖

The Cream Separator

By Edna Clou

The undulating whir and whine of the cream separator floated into our kitchen. Dad was separating already! With tin cup in hand and curls flying, I ran to the milk house. I hoped I wasn't too late!

I tried to edge between Dad and the pails of foaming separated milk. At that moment he leaned backward. Next thing I knew I was sitting, bottom first, in a pail of milk! Milk flew in all directions as my chunky body pretty well filled the pail! Milk in my eyes, my hair, my apron pockets—I was drenched! To make matters worse, Dad laughed—and how he laughed—as he pulled me from the pail.

All sticky and smelling like a cow, I stomped to the house and into Grandmother's arms. I just knew he intended to push me, when in fact he didn't know I was around. I was satisfied, though, when Grandmother said, "What on earth did you do to this child?"

From that time on, I had an aversion to cream separators. Mounted on an iron frame was a tank for milk. Beneath the faucet was a little cup with a float and, beneath that, a spout each for milk and cream. In the center was a whirling bowl that separated the cream from the milk by centrifugal force. Before separating began, the handle had to be turned until the bowl spun at the proper speed. Turning the separator by hand took a strong back and arms. After milking those cows by hand and turning the separator, the farmer really earned his cream check.

But there was a woman's part in this cream check too, as I soon learned. The blessed thing had to be spotlessly clean in order to get Grade A price from the Sutherland Creamery.

This was one of the very first morning tasks—washing that separator before it soured. Mother soon had me rinsing it first with cold water to remove the milk before a hot suds bath. If I failed to rinse it all off, the hot wash became a slippery, ropy, sticky, smelly mess—enough to turn your stomach!

Next came the wash in hot suds. Inside the revolving bowl were 35 fine metal discs. They fit together so precisely, they were numbered. Each had to be put on the spindle in correct order. For washing and airing they were slipped onto a large wire frame, much like an

Before separating began, the handle had to be turned until the bowl spun at the proper speed.

oversized safety pin. Here, too, is where rinsing with cold water first was really needed. If these got sour milk between them, they would stick together—and that sour smell!

Then came the heavy bowl that fit over the discs. Usually it collected about one-third inch of dirt, scum and whatnot inside. I used to grimace as I took my finger and scraped it out separately.

Then there was a large screen strainer and that blessed strainer cloth! If not carefully rinsed and washed, the strainer cloth would become stiff with old milk and be smelly and useless.

After all this suds washing, next came a teakettle of boiling water to scald the whole process, spouts and all. Usually we placed the bowl and parts in a sunny place to air, with a clean dishtowel pinned over to keep out flies.

Speaking of flies, wonder what folks today would do if they saw all the flies we did? The barn rafters would be black with them at milking time. Even when the milk pails were covered, some would manage to fall in and be strained out with that strainer cloth.

Oh! No, we aren't through washing yet— those milk pails, inside and especially outside! Sometimes an old cow became restless and something with a greenish cast was left on the outside of the pail as she tried to kick! That had to be washed off first, in separate water to be sure! And the "ears" of the pail where the handles were fastened—there was a perfect spot for yellow scum to form. Better not be found there by Dad!

Oh, yes, and that iron separator frame and the floor around it! Somehow in its whirling frenzy, the innards would leak out separator oil, combined with a little spilled milk. Whew! That frame had to shine—and no spilled milk on the floor!

So, when I was married and a farmer's wife, I insisted the separator be set up in my big kitchen. There it was handy to hot water, free from dust and away from flies. With the coming of the Rural Electrification Administration, power made separating much easier.

Still there was another task. After walking to the pasture to bring in the cows for evening

PRICES REDUCED $15
on all
McCORMICK-DEERING
Cream Separators

FARM FAMILIES with an eye for economy can't afford to overlook the $15 price reduction on all six sizes of McCormick-Deering Cream Separators.

McCormick-Deering Cream Separators have been value leaders in their field for many years. Now, with this reduction, they are a better buy than ever. They have the famous McCormick-Deering features that give you *close skimming, easy turning, easy washing,* and *durability.*

Ask the McCormick-Deering dealer to show you this separator with STAINLESS STEEL DISKS that wear longer, resist cracking, do not rust. Buy a new McCormick-Deering at this new, low price . . . get the benefits of its smooth, quiet, trouble-free operation. The dealer near you will also be glad to tell you about the line of McCormick-Deering Milkers and Milk Coolers.

INTERNATIONAL HARVESTER COMPANY
(INCORPORATED)
180 North Michigan Avenue   Chicago, Illinois

In This Machine You Get:
✔ CLOSE SKIMMING
✔ EASY TURNING
✔ EASY WASHING
✔ DURABILITY

McCORMICK-DEERING
MILK COOLERS • MILKERS • CREAM SEPARATORS

milking, I'd rush in and put the separator together. Each part had to be assembled just right, especially the heavy screw top to the bowl that held the discs. My husband was glad to see the separator ready to go as he lugged in two or three huge pails of milk from the barn.

The cream ran out its spout into a tall can provided by the creamery. A truck picked up cream three times a week. It was a pleasant change to visit with our cream man and sometimes share a cup of coffee on a frigid winter's day.

Creamery men often told us of strange objects found in cream. One of the most unusual was a pair of baby shoes.

Those cream checks bought food, clothing and provided for family needs.

Skimmed milk was fed to calves and pigs mostly. Often I'd ask for a pail and make a big stone crock of cottage cheese.

Cream cans and old separators are intrigues today. Often we see an old separator in the yard, the tank filled with flowers; or a cream can in a modern living room, used for an umbrella rack.

Somehow, I just don't get excited over them—not at all! ❖

WINTER VACATION?   NOT ON THIS FARM

The tractor on this farm spends the nights in the barn. But not the days, either winter or sum-
mer. For it is a working tractor—working four full seasons a year—wherever there is work to
be done. It's a Ford Tractor with Ferguson System. It doesn't demand a winter vacation.

On your farm, winter may not bring cold and snow. But still the farm year is a twelve-month year, especially if you're going to handle those "when-I-get-time" jobs. You can make the season between crops mighty profitable, if you have the right equipment.

There are lots of good tractors made nowadays. Many of them are three-wheel jobs—cultivating machines. They do good work, but they're specialists. Big trouble is, they are not easily suited to do *all* the work on your farm.

Compare one of those machines with the Ford Tractor with Ferguson System.

It won't take you long to see the advantage of four-wheel stability, of automobile type easy steering, of quick adaptability to one job after another, with implements changed in a minute or less.

Then, there is the Ferguson System—a new method of attaching implements and controlling them in the ground—making implement and tractor a complete, easy-to-operate unit.

That makes this lightweight, economical tractor a tough competitor in the middleweight class, without asking you to buy extra weight, or drag it around the farm.

Pull two 14-inch plows, or a big two-gang disc, cultivate a section or a kitchen garden, mow heavy crops, break new ground—it's all the same to the Ford Tractor with Ferguson System. The System does it—makes this tractor different from all others—gets more work out

of a gallon of gas than you ever thought possible.

It will help you get all of your regular farm planting and cultivating and harvesting done *on time*. That's important. And then it's ready to do the off-season jobs—clearing, cutting wood, filling silos, grinding feed, pumping water, farm hauling—whatever you want done.

This four-wheel, four-season equipment is ready to go at the touch of the starter, lets you off easy on gas and oil, and asks no questions about the kind of job you want it to do next. The boys can run it, too, or for that matter, the girls.

Sounds like a big contract, but you'll believe it when you see a demonstration, right on your own farm. The nearest Ford Tractor Dealer will gladly take care of that for you.

The Ford Tractor with Ferguson System is sold nationally by the Ferguson-Sherman Manufacturing Corporation, Dearborn, Michigan, and distributed through dealers in every part of the country.

Old Red

By Frances Wolfe

It was like saying goodbye to an old friend to say goodbye to Old Red. Perhaps I'd better explain: Old Red was our 1936 W-30 tractor.

She had plowed many a mile of ground and prepared it for planting. Discing—now there's where Old Red excelled in plowing her furrows straight. It was a pretty sight to watch her; steadily rumbling up and down the field she'd go, never uttering a complaint.

In the winter, when cars, trucks and other means of transportation refused to budge, the call came: "Bring Old Red and give me a pull." If it was too cold for the car to start or if someone got stuck, "Get Old Red. She'll pull me out."

Her paint began to peel and she began to look like her working days were over. But just as a lady feels revitalized with a new hat, a coat of paint did the same for Old Red. We gave her a complete overhaul of sleeves, pistons and rings, and it kept her purring mile after mile.

When she pulled a pull-type combine and the ground was the least bit muddy, slowly lumbering through the mud they'd go. It was a sad day for Old Red when the self-propelled combine came in style. It was the beginning of the end for Old Red; one less job to do.

Came the day when parts were hard to find; finally it got down to the point that the only parts available were used parts. Old Red felt humiliated, but the old girl suffered the used parts to be used, and as usual she did her job with a willing carburetor to assist her. No complaints were heard from her; she just minded her own business and plodded along.

Finally Old Red became tired, sluggish and moved slower and slower. Her rings fouled up; her sleeves became loose; she began to complain. The words "No parts available" signaled the end. Something now had to be done.

After looking at a lot of other tractors, we found one which we thought could replace Old Red. It was a diesel job, but not Old Red. The diesel's capacity for oil was like the thirst of a thirsty man; she gulped down quarts compared to Old Red. Her rows were not quite straight, and her work was done under grumbling and protest.

After looking at a lot of other tractors, we found one which we thought could replace Old Red. It was a diesel job, but not Old Red. The diesel's capacity for oil was like the thirst of a thirsty man; she gulped down quarts compared to Old Red. Her rows were not quite straight, and her work was done under grumbling and protest.

Old Red is gone. We miss her and we know that she will be going as strong as she can, till the last horsepower is gone and she comes to a halting, stumbling stop.

The miles she traveled were good ones and now, no more. Gee! We still miss Old Red—the best W-30 in the world.

Here's to you, Old Red, whatever junkyard you're in. We miss you, ✤

Treasure Trove

By Lydia S. Miller

I was the eighth in a family of nine children and, since my mother was always busy with the baby or helping an older sister or brother, I spent most of my time trailing behind Grandma and Grandpa. I helped them with whatever they were doing. The two places that stand out most vividly in my memory are Grandpa's smokehouse and Grandma's cellar.

The little 12-foot-by-15-foot smokehouse in the back yard was built of logs, complete with a dirt floor and no windows. In lieu of a ceiling, several oak poles ran overhead from wall to wall. From the poles hung shoulders, hams, two or three flitches of bacon and loops of link sausage, all in varying stages of curing by the smoke from a hickory fire on the dirt floor.

Whenever I see a baked ham or sausage these days, I recall how much work went on behind the scenes before ham or sausage was brought to our dinner table.

The only furnishings in the smokehouse were a rough board table and a huge wooden salting box with a covered barrel beside it. Along the other wall were several crocks of various sizes.

After Papa, with some hired help, killed, dressed and cut up the hog or hogs, Grandpa and Grandma carried on from there. What delicious food they prepared and stored for us!

I can just see Grandpa "trimming up" the sides, hams, shoulders and other cuts, tossing the leaner trimmings into the sausage crock, and fat and skin into the soap grease crock. Then he would pack the pieces in the salting box with thick layers of salt between. After he'd covered the top layer of meat with salt, he'd spread a clean cloth over it and place the heavy box lid in place on the box. Then it was on to making sausage.

To the trimmings crock he'd add some shoulder and even tenderloin, grind it all up together and add sage, salt and red and black pepper. If Grandma had the sausage casing made up from the hog's entrails, he'd stuff them for link sausage. But he'd leave some bulk sausage for

Grandma's special sausage fry.

Grandpa would say, "Go get an egg— and be sure you wash it," and I'd dash away, hurrying to get back and watch him wash the barrel and lid, fill it with well water, and pour in salt and stir and stir to dissolve the salt. When the brine was strong enough to float the clean egg, he would drop in some strips of shoulder, a tongue and the pigs feet Grandma had cleaned. He covered the barrel.

He would help Grandma with her chores; then, after about 10 days, he would dip all the brine out of the barrel and boil it in the big old black wash pot. He would skim it several times, then pour it back over the meat, cover it and let it set to cure.

When the time was right, Grandpa would take the meat from the salt box, wipe off each piece and hang it up to begin curing alongside the link sausage. No vestal virgin ever tended the fires in the temple of Diana more faithfully than he did his hickory fire for curing. He had a reputation for being the best sausage maker for miles around; he had to protect that reputation.

Whenever I see a baked ham or sausage these days, I recall how much work went on behind the scenes before ham or sausage was brought to our dinner table. I never could decide whether I liked Grandpa's smoked link sausage or Grandma's sausage patties best.

I'd stand beside her as she fried a skillet (spider, she called it) full of sausage patties. She would put a layer of cooked patties in a crock then pour the hot grease over them, fry another batch and cover with the grease until all her sausage was used. When cold, she'd cover the crock with a clean white cloth and heavy lid, and that was ready for the cellar.

I never wanted to miss Grandma's hogshead cheese or souse making. When she had boiled the cleaned hog head with some backbone and some of Grandpa's trimmings until the meat fell off the bones, she would poke around in the pot with a long-handle fork and lift out the large bones. After the meat cooled, she would wash her hands and feel around in the pot for any little bitty bones. She'd add red and black pepper, rubbed sage, and minced garlic to taste—always she seasoned to taste. I never recall seeing her measure a teaspoon of this or that.

With the souse cooling, Grandma would spoon out a little dish of it for me and one for her. Sitting on a high stool, she'd taste and nod her head, for it was just right. Then the souse was poured into a clean cloth sack and hung up over a dripping pan. When it was cold, Grandma would scrape the hardened grease off the sack, adding that to the soap grease supply, and dump the souse from the sack into a crock. She would weight it down with a heavy plate, cover it, and the crock was ready for cellar storage. Sometimes she made pans of scrapple, too.

But when Grandma turned to the tub of hog entrails, I stepped back, pinching my nose. They didn't smell so good. When she had trimmed off the fat for soap grease, she washed the entrails out. She'd cut them into smaller pieces for easier handling, and some way she turned each piece inside out on a smooth oak rod. She would spread each piece across the wash block and scrape one side and then the other. After soaking the cleaned entrails in soda water, then rinsing them several times, she set some of the clean, strong, paper-thin entrails aside for Grandpa's sausage casing, and the remainder went into a pot to boil all day for chitterlings. The "chitlins," when properly cooked and served with hot sauce, are delicious, as anyone will tell you who learned to like them before he was old enough to know better.

When all her crocks were ready, Grandpa came to take them to the cellar. I trailed along, and sometimes Grandma took pans of scrapple she had made.

The cellar was under the kitchen but the only door was outside facing the smokehouse. On the hottest days it was cool and pleasant inside, and at the cold hog-killing season it was cozy and warm. There was an unforgettable smell of mellowing apples comingled with the clean odor of lye soap and fresh buttermilk. Along one wall was the milk safe—high, chestlike, with doors and sides partly of tin with tiny holes to air-cool the milk. Inside were shelves filled with crocks of milk, earthen jugs of buttermilk and molds of apple-and-leaf–imprinted pounds of butter.

Along the other wall were two oaken barrels of ribbon sugar cane syrup and Grandma's churn, guarded by old Barney, the toad that sat there, its front feet pigeon-toed, staring with pop eyes at all intruders. But Barney kept the cellar free of insects! To the rows of crocks Grandpa added the crocks of sausage and souse alongside those containing sauerkraut and pickles.

When he remarked that the lye hominy crock was empty, Grandma said, "If you chaps will shell corn Friday, we can make lye hominy Saturday."

That was one thing I did like to help do. My job was to keep poking wood into the fire, for hominy making took lots of hot water. I can still smell the clean odor of burning oak and see those huge three-legged black wash pots that straddled orange flames licking and swirling this way and that in the gusting wind.

I can still hear the screaking pulley and the bang-clanging of the long zinc well bucket as my brother let it down into the well to draw water. It was his task to keep those wash pots full, and I was glad I didn't have to turn the windlass, winding up the rope as it drew bucket after bucket of water.

> *I can still hear the screaking pulley and the bang-clanging of the long zinc well bucket as my brother let it down into the well to draw water.*

Nothing was wasted. All year, oak ashes were put into a barrel atop a low slanting platform. Beneath the platform's lower edge, a porcelain pan caught lye drippings, formed when rain drenched those ashes. So, when my fire had the big wash pot boiling, Grandma added some of the coffee-colored lye to the hot water. She then boiled the corn in the mixture until the husks easily slipped off the plump grains. She'd rinse and boil the cleaned corn in clear salt water until it was all lye- and husk-free. Usually there were two crocks filled with our lye hominy.

When Grandpa took those crocks to the cellar, that was our last winter storage task, and when sleet covered the ground and every little tree twig was cellophaned in ice, a supper of sauerkraut and sausage patties from Grandma's cellar, or ham from Grandpa's smokehouse—oh my, that was good eating!

What a treasure trove—Grandpa's smokehouse and Grandma's cellar. ❖

The Coming of Winter

By Hazle M. Convey

It wasn't too long ago when the coming of winter was the signal for all hands to "heave ho" and make ready. It all began in the early spring when, on Good Friday, the potatoes were put in the ground. From then on, the preparation increased progressively, until at last it reached its feverish crescendo at harvest time.

From the spring—when your back felt like a matchstick ready to crack as you bent over the strawberry patch (though it helped to remember that you'd relish the jam next January on your breakfast pancakes)—to the fall—when you followed the horse-drawn plow which gouged into the brown, dry dirt and upturned hundreds of hills of potatoes—the thought of the coming cold upheld and propelled you.

It wasn't too long ago when the coming of winter was the signal for all hands to "heave ho" and make ready.

Doggedly you stooped to gather the potatoes and put them into an old gunnysack held between you and a partner. The turned-up earth was hard and full of clods that hurt the bare feet, and the dry dusty potatoes were most unpleasant to the touch, but you ignored the knife in the small of your back and envisioned heaping bowls of snowy mashed potatoes while the machine that was you mechanically picked and automatically tossed the spuds in the sack.

And during all the trying times and chores in between, winter's demands prorated those any child might have.

Did you ever pit bushels and bushels of cherries, cherry by cherry, until you swore you'd never eat another one for the rest of your life? In the sweltering heat of a July afternoon, when the salty sweat ran down through your brows and made your eyes smart—along with a few tears of exasperation—you longed to wriggle in the "crick" along with the tadpoles and bullheads, or to just lie on its mossy bank and watch the dragonfly airplanes zooming back and forth above the water. But, no, the red mountain of cherries loomed there before you, and you pitted away the day—hands and arms stained crimson, juice stinging in the places where you'd scratched mosquito bites the night before.

You attacked equally enormous amounts of peaches and pears and apricots and, somehow, you got through it all—the scrubbing and sterilizing of jars and lids, the picking and peeling and packing of fruit. The old kitchen range became a monster, consuming cobs by the carload; as fast as her belly went empty it had to be filled. It took a lot of cooking and canning to be sure that our own bellies would be filled in the winter to come. The tons of tomatoes and gallons of gherkins became relentless rulers of time as they, too, rushed into season.

Golden carrots were buried in great stone crocks full of sand and stored in the outdoor cellar, along with those bushels and bushels of potatoes you'd helped to pick. Barrels of shiny red Jonathans for eating, plus other apples for cooking, stood off to one side of the cave; and on the opposite end, on shelf after shelf from floor to ceiling, row upon row of glass Mason jars held the fruits and vegetables to which you had literally dedicated your life in the preceding seasons. Light coming in from the air hole overhead sent off a multicolored gleam from the jam and jelly gems in their round little glasses with the paraffin hats. They were our jewels for January, February and March—and all the days ahead!

Did you ever open a cave and descend into its cool, musty sanctity? Did you ever fling open the inner door to almost feel, as well as smell, the musky odor of the foods therein mingled with that of the dank dark clay? This, coupled with the sight of the stores within, made you feel warm and safe inside, and spelled security with a capital S! Surely the cave of Ali Baba and his 40 thieves held no jewels to compare with those cached away in our dugout!

The little, gray, weather-beaten smokehouse on the back of the lot housed its own treasure of home-cured hams and bacon. The smells emanating from it conjured up such delightful visions as buckwheat pancakes dripping melted butter and enhancing platters of succulent smoked meats. One sniff of the ham sent your pylorus dancing, and your mouth watered at thoughts of the repasts ahead—bountiful baked-ham dinners; thick, nourishing bean soup cooked with the bone from the ham; golden mounds of scrambled eggs complementing hearty slices of that delicate pink meat with its subtle flavor; or, better still, eggs served with generous rashers of the homegrown bacon which had a flavor store-bought bacon can never achieve!

Upstairs in our house, in an extra room known as the storeroom, were huge sacks of dried beans and peas which had been laboriously threshed by hand. Dangling above them, summer sausages swung from the rafters, suspended on lengths of binder's twine. Many other good things were stored away there, including food for the soul as well as the body. Bunches of brilliantly hued strawflowers and stalks of cockscomb, hanging upside down, were being dried for winter bouquets—Mama's touch of beauty for winter-weary eyes!

Strands of onions, their stems braided together, hung out in the granary; and the bins of wheat and oats yielded up squashes and pumpkins for winter pies.

When the cob bin was full and the stack of firewood for the range grew higher and higher as the days grew

shorter and shorter, and when the frost crept in stealthily on a clear, cold night, it was not yet time to cease the activity. No, frost was merely the signal that the butchering could commence, to add good fresh meat to the accumulated provender. Nature's was the only deep-freeze in those busy days and, as in all else, her whims dictated our moves.

When at last the north wind did come in earnest, blowing the swirling, dancing snow into a cover that blanketed the labored land for its earned winter rest, we too could rest, our labors done—for a little while, at least—until February, when the spring butchering and the summer sausage took over again! We could

greet the season with open arms and hearts that were glad.

We were through getting ready for the coming of winter, for it was here; and we could enjoy it because we were prepared. Because we had done it ourselves, we could sit back with that feeling of inner satisfaction that comes only from a job well done. It is man's natural-born instinct, like the rest of the animal kingdom, to prepare himself for the winter ahead; and when he does his job well, he is at peace with himself and with God.

Man, in his inventive genius, has deprived himself of many joys; and preparing for the coming of winter is one of them. ✣

Wash Day

By Elinor L. Brown

Wash day on the farm when I was a child was a day to remember. Monday was as religiously observed for wash day as Sunday was for the Sabbath.

Many times preparations for the day were made the night before. We placed the boiler under the pump spout and hand-pumped water into it until it was about a third full. Two of us carried the boiler of water into the house and lifted it to the top of the cookstove. We finished filling the boiler with buckets of water.

On Monday morning, Mother arose early to start the fire in the stove, burning cobs and wood to heat the water to nearly boiling. When the water was partially hot, Mother would put in part of a can of lye to "break" the water, as we called it. This created a scum on top of the water which was lime and other materials or dirt. This was skimmed off, then homemade lye soap was added. In the summertime we washed on the porch, so this meant dipping water out of the boiler and carrying it safely to fill the washing machine.

Nearly regardless of the weather, the clothes were hung outdoors. In the winter, Mother always depended on them to freeze dry.

We kids had to stay around close to take our turns powering the washing machine. We filled the rinse tubs with clear, cold water from the well and the washing was ready to start. The machine was loaded, first with white clothes that were the least soiled. The machine was the kind with a semicircular tub, with a handle in the center for tossing the machine back and forth to develop suction within it.

It was a tiring chore to toss the machine back and forth for about 15 minutes for each load of clothes. The clothes were then put through the hand-turned wringer into the rinse waters. By the time five or six loads of clothes were washed through the wash water and rinsed, the last ones conveyed a tint of tattletale gray.

The best clothes were hung on the clothesline, but the overalls and dark clothes usually ended up flung over the garden fence.

Nearly regardless of the weather, the clothes were hung outdoors. In the winter, Mother always depended on them to freeze dry. She would bring them in, frozen nearly stiff as boards sometimes, and hang them on backs of chairs in front of the oven or around the potbellied heating stove. We had no basement to hang them in.

If the weather was cooperative, Mother tried to iron much of the flat work on wash day. This meant building a hot fire in cold or hot weather and heating the irons on top of the stove. She would remove one iron at a time with a wooden-handled clamp and iron fast before the iron got cold and had to be exchanged for a hot one. We usually tested the iron on a piece of paper to be sure it wasn't too hot.

For many, many years, Mother did not have an ironing board, and how she longed for one. She ironed on a padded table leaf on top of the dining-room table.

Those were days when wash day took a lot of energy and little thought was given to social activities. Most of the time and physical energies were expended in the daily work of housekeeping and caring for the family. ❖

Give your washing-machine the benefit of naptha

Real naptha—that marvelous dirt-loosener used by professional dry-cleaners—cannot be obtained in prepared-flake form. The only way, therefore, to give your washing-machine the benefit of naptha is to make your own Fels-Naptha flakes (or soap-paste) as needed, on washday. Do this for cleaner clothes.

Wet the clothes; and either shave the Fels-Naptha directly into the washing-machine, or make a soap paste (using your usual amount of soap); let them soak a few minutes. The real naptha will go through every thread, loosen the dirt for the sudsy water to flush away, then vanish—leaving the clothes clean, sweet, sanitary.

No matter *how* you wash clothes, Fels-Naptha will wash them cleaner, more quickly, safely and thoroughly. For Fels-Naptha is *more* than soap. It is *more* than soap and naptha. It is the exclusive Fels-Naptha blend of splendid soap and real naptha in a way that brings out the best in these two great cleaners. Directions inside every wrapper.

TEST Fels-Naptha's wonderful efficiency. Send 2c in stamps for sample bar. Address Fels-Naptha Soap, Philadelphia.

Real naptha! You can tell by the smell

"Farm wives are enthusiastic about the way Fels-Naptha cleans and sweetens milk pails, strainers, separators and other dairy utensils. "No other soap like Fels-Naptha", says one."

The original and genuine naptha soap, in the red-and-green wrapper.

FELS-NAPTHA
THE GOLDEN BAR WITH THE CLEAN NAPTHA ODOR

Annable